More Praise for *Smart Calling*

"Smart Calling is the benchmark as the highest professional standard for effective cold calling. Take the initiative to read and implement Art's rational principles and you will sell much more and develop a prospect base of potential customers that will call you when they are ready to purchase or graciously take your future calls. This is *the best* sales text I have read in the past 20 years."

—**Rex Caswell, PhD, Vice President,**
Sales Effectiveness BI Worldwide

"The book is tremendous, and I think you are brilliant. I probably highlighted half of it! I am recommending it to my clients as a must-read.

—**Mike Weinberg, Author of *New Sales. Simplified,***
www.NewSalesCoach.com

"Your book changed my professional life. I have my Smart research down to a science and produce about three leads every hour."

—**Sam Shenker, Associated Global Systems**

"I've been using the phone to sell for seven years, and before I picked up Art's *Smart Calling* book I thought I knew it all. But after reading through the first few chapters I quickly realized that I knew nothing. Just the section on call openings and voice mails has transformed my career and skyrocketed my results to new levels. This book is a *must* for anyone serious about selling over the phone. Art really delivers."

—**Shane Varcoe, Regional Sales Manager**

"Art Sobczak understands the difference between direct marketing and cold-calling, which many sales gurus simply don't. *Smart Calling* is a phenomenal resource for anyone that truly wants to excel in sales. The advice is obviously from experience, and Mr. Sobczak offers sound techniques that everyone could use."

—**Chris Lott, VP of Sales, DataTel Communications**

"Art doesn't tell us what to do without also telling us how to do it. For sellers that are trying to improve their success on the phone, Art Sobczak has written the definitive book."

—**Tim Rohrer, SalesAndMarketingLoudmouth.com**

SMART
CALLING

SMART CALLING

Eliminate the Fear, Failure,
and Rejection from Cold Calling

Second Edition

ART SOBCZAK

WILEY

Cover design: Paul McCarthy

Published by John Wiley & Sons, Inc., Hoboken, New Jersey.
Published simultaneously in Canada.

For general information about our other products and services, please contact our Customer Care Department within the United States at (800) 762-2974, outside the United States at (317) 572-3993, or fax (317) 572-4002.

Wiley publishes in a variety of print and electronic formats and by print-on-demand. Some material included with standard print versions of this book may not be included in e-books or in print-on-demand. If this book refers to media such as a CD or DVD that is not included in the version you purchased, you may download this material at http://booksupport.wiley.com. For more information about Wiley products, visit www.wiley.com.

Library of Congress Cataloging-in-Publication Data:

Sobczak, Art.
    Smart calling : eliminate the fear, failure, and rejection from cold calling / Art Sobczak. — 2nd Edition.
        pages   cm
    Includes bibliographical references and index.
    ISBN 978-1-118-58871-0 (cloth); ISBN 978-1-118-63740-1 (ebk);
    ISBN 978-1-118-63751-7 (ebk); ISBN 978-1-118-63738-8 (ebk)
        1. Telephone selling.   2. Telemarketing.   I. Title.
    HF5438.3.S63   2013
    658.8′72—dc23
                                                                            2012049854

Printed in the United States of America
10 9 8 7 6

CONTENTS

INTRODUCTION

When I first wrote this book three years ago, I had a feeling it would do pretty well. After all, I had been teaching the same things in my public and in-company training programs for years, and the process and material was field-tested. What actually happened blew me away.

We hit Number One in the Sales category on Amazon.com on the very first day. It stayed there for a while, and it continues to sell well three years later, while hundreds of other sales books have died on the vine. It was named Top Sales Book of 2010 by Top Sales Awards, beating out some other very fine books by big-time sales authors. And the reviews and success stories from people who use the process to get results have been both gratifying and humbling.

If you are reading *Smart Calling* for the first time, welcome aboard! If you have been through the original, welcome back. While I've added some additional examples, tips, techniques, and success stories from readers, the process itself hasn't changed. But the reason I wanted to do this second edition is because of what *has* changed in the past few years: our ability to Smarten up our calls, making it even easier to be successful. You'll see many of these updates in Chapter 5.

So, what's this Smart Calling stuff all about?

Let's go back a few years. Okay, a lot of years. I wish I had had this book when I first got out of college and into my first corporate sales job with AT&T in 1982. It would have prevented a lot of grief and made me much more money.

Then again, some of it would not have made sense, since there was no Internet and PCs were just making their appearance. And "sales intelligence" meant going to the library and finding a list of businesses that belonged to a trade association. However, even without the benefit of today's technology, the pure prospecting and sales process and techniques in this book would have worked 30 years ago, just as they do today and will 30 years from now and beyond.

Even in the numerous sales jobs I had in high school and college, I knew that typical cold calling—phoning people I didn't know anything about and giving a pitch—didn't make sense and was actually quite painful. I always tried to find a better way, an edge that would get superior results; I was constantly reading, listening to tapes, attending seminars, studying, and tinkering with my own approach. I always did well in my sales positions. However, I also knew I would never be good enough for my satisfaction and that there always is more to learn. My quest continued in a couple of other corporate sales jobs and then in my own company as I had to pound the phones to acquire clients for my fledgling consulting and training firm.

Eventually, I did find—and continue to fine-tune—a better way. You are holding it (or reading it on your screen): a smarter way to prospect. A process that makes sense and gets results, and one that does not require you to sound like that cheesy salesperson that everyone considers an intrusive pest.

This book is a step-by-step guide that will show you how to call people you do not know and who do not know you, engage them in a conversation, and ultimately get them to take some action. And in the cases where you do not accomplish that primary objective, I will show you how to avoid the morale-killing rejection that is usually associated with telephone prospecting.

I've built my business and reputation over the past 30 years on delivering very specific how-to tactics and strategies. Many people—including, unfortunately, sales trainers and authors—tell you what you *should* do on the phone. You *should* create interest. You *should* get past the screener. You *should* leave a compelling voice mail message. And listeners and readers say, "Uh, okay," as they wonder *how* in the heck they are going to do it. I'll answer that for you and give you a precise recipe and ingredients for prospecting success by phone.

This book is long on practical how-tos and short on big picture strategy and fluff. I've always been somewhat of a simple, get-to-the-point kind of guy—a style you'll see and from which you'll benefit throughout this book. What I've learned from delivering more than 1,300 training sessions and studying human behavior and learning styles, is that people learn best when you relate to their world and entertain them. Therefore, you will see many examples of stories as I make my points.

I will guide you through the logical creation and execution of your own telephone prospecting call using my Smart Call methodology. You will learn the same process and techniques I present to my training clients. These methods are being used successfully to initiate profitable relationships worldwide, and I'm confident they can work for you, too, just like the thousands who have already read this book and made it part of their sales process.

Unlike some gurus out there, I don't claim to have invented sales, and I certainly don't have all the answers. I don't believe that my approach is the only way to realize success. That's why I will give examples from and point you in the direction of others with expertise in some very specific aspects of sales—and others with a more generalist view—throughout this book.

You may not agree with everything I say. I don't care. Actually, that is good, since it means you are thinking about what you read and applying it to your situation. That is healthy. What I do ask is that when you do disagree, react as you should when you get resistance in a sales situation and ask yourself, *How might this be true?* or *How could this work for me?*

Who Will Benefit from Smart Calling?

The primary audience, of course, is all people with "sales" in their title, primarily those who sell to other businesses. But it's not limited to traditional salespeople. Anyone who picks up the phone to call a person they don't know—with the objective of persuading that person to take some action—will learn from this book. For example:

- Freelancers of all types
- Independent professionals
- Sports recruiters
- Writers looking to get published
- Job seekers
- Fund raisers
- Many others

Regardless of whether your career relies on regularly calling people to get new business or whether you have one person to whom you want to sell an idea and may never place a prospecting call again, this book will help you do what is necessary.

Taking Action Is Required

As I tell my training workshop participants, everything I will share with you is totally worthless—until you *do* something with it. I know this material works, but only if *you* do.

My friend Larry Winget—who is known as an irritational motivational speaker—says in his book *It's Called Work for a Reason—Success Is Your Own Damn Fault* that many people are "spectators rather than doers." I agree, and I have seen too much evidence of that among the ranks of salespeople who do nothing to improve themselves—even when the resources are provided to them. I'm hopeful that is not you. You have taken the first step by investing in this book. The payoff will now come by putting in the work.

There are a number of exercises throughout the book that ask you to research, write, and practice. At the end of each chapter, I also ask what other action you will commit to as a result of that chapter.

Prospecting and sales is a lot like golf: You can read all you want to and become knowledgeable about it, but you will become excellent at it only by practicing. I know it sounds like a cliché, but you will get out of this book what you put into it.

I'm ready if you are. Let's begin making your prospecting calls Smart!

SECTION
ONE

The Smart Calling Concept

Cold Calling Is Dumb, but Prospecting Is Necessary

Smart Calling Is the Answer

Cold calling.

Just hearing the words whispered causes chest-tightening, loss-of-breath anxiety for many people.

Perhaps one of these people is you. And maybe that's why you're reading this. Given the choice, most people would rather have their fingernails slowly removed with pliers than pick up the phone, call someone they do not know, and try to persuade them to do—or buy—something.

The mere notion of cold calling arouses fear—which results in most people's reluctance to do it. Add that to the fact that many cold callers lack the knowledge and ability to do it well—not knowing any better than to use the cheesy, sleazy, salesy-sounding techniques that have spread like viruses over the years—and it further compounds the ultimate feelings of rejection after failing.

Yes, making cold calls is distasteful. And it's dumb. I suggest you never place another one. In fact, after finishing this book, I want you to banish the term from your vocabulary when referring to professional telephone prospecting.

But how will you know what never to do again? Let's begin by defining a cold call.

A cold call takes place when a salesperson calls someone he does not know, who does not know him, and—having little or no information on the prospect—robotically dials number after number, giving the same pitch to everyone who answers.

Of course, these calls are destined for failure. To illustrate the absurdity of the concept, let's look at this scenario:

A magazine writer is assigned an interview with Brad Pitt. He begins his conversation with the world-renowned movie personality by saying: "So, Brad, I'm going to do the same type of interview I've done with hundreds of other people. Now—what is it *exactly* that you do?"

Ridiculous, right? Such a scenario would *never* take place.

Now imagine this: A sales rep phones a company, gets someone she believes to be a decision maker on the phone, and says, "Hi, I'm Erin Nelson with Able Supply, a company that sells maintenance supplies. I'd like to tell you about our products and talk about becoming a vendor for you. Now—what is it that your company does?"

Though equally absurd, conversations like these occur every day: unprepared salespeople blindly make phone calls, using tired, old-school sales techniques, *hoping* that because they picked up the phone and made a call they will find someone who will agree to what they want to accomplish.

But hoping is clearly not enough.

Why Telephone Prospecting Is Both Essential and Profitable

Now that we have thoroughly trashed the concept of cold calling, let's get something else perfectly clear: Telephone prospecting is essential for business sustainability and growth.

Huh?

That's right. Prospecting by phone is a *necessary* part of new business acquisition and growth.

Ideally, it's not the only way, but it's a vital component of the model. Businesses that merely react—waiting for the phone to ring, for web orders to stream in, and on business coming from existing customers—are not nearly as successful as those who employ proactive hunting, or telephone prospecting, as part of the mix.

Think about it: Every business has customers who quit buying for lots of reasons—bankruptcy, downsizing, switching vendors, death, lack of attention from the vendor, and more. Therefore, you need to replace that business just to stay even—and then hope to grow. And telephone prospecting can do that for you—quickly.

Of course, it needs to be done in the right way; the Smart Calling way, as we'll discuss soon.

Oh, there are detractors out there, people who say—and even believe—that prospecting is dead. They use the term *cold calling* in their denouncements, but they mean phone prospecting in general. Some of these anti-cold-calling gurus have made names for themselves and profited by preying on the fear of cold calling. Just look at some of the books and learning programs released over the past few years:

Cold Calling Is Obsolete
No More Cold Calling
Never Cold Call Again

These resources suggest either getting people to refer you to decision makers, creating social media and inbound marketing strategies, or doing old-fashioned direct marketing to generate leads so that people contact you. Those are sound theories and certainly preferable to cold calling. If you have the time, ability, and money to engage in those types of marketing programs to generate leads, I suggest you take advantage of them. They all work, and smart companies realize that there are many spokes to the wheel that results in new business. I use them all myself. In fact, I have personally generated millions of dollars in sales from direct response advertising—a process wherein people with whom I have never spoken simply placed orders with us, over the phone, through the mail and online, and gave me money.

However, in reality, all these forms of marketing are just that: marketing. And when a sales rep—whose primary job is to *sell*—spends precious selling time sending out letters, drafting e-mails, putting out door hangers, posting on social media sites, and completing other administrative busywork, then he is avoiding his most important function: talking to people. I've seen many sales reps who thought they were being productive by sending out mail. In fact, they were just busy. In many instances, they were afraid to make the calls, so they deluded themselves into believing that they were engaging in sales behavior, which, in actuality, was avoidance behavior.

I love the environment we operate within today. As I'll discuss later, social intelligence makes it so easy to place a Smart Call. And many forms of social media make it easier to connect. But this is not selling. There is an element of hope that someone will reach out and contact you.

Mike Weinberg, author of the great book *New Sales. Simplified* (get it, a wonderful complement to this one) says so perfectly,

"Sales is a verb."

He adds,

"Top performers in sales don't wait for anything or anyone."

"Top performers act."

"Waiting is the key for new business failure."

I couldn't agree more. When you have identified a prospect you feel would be a great customer—someone you just know would benefit wildly from a business relationship—you may very well grow old and poor waiting for that person to respond to a marketing campaign. And you might not know anyone who could refer you to her. But picking up the phone quickly fixes all of that.

The fact—proven by those of us who have made fortunes doing it and those showing success right now—is that prospecting by phone *works*. And when done the *right* way—the Smart Calling way (oops, jumping ahead again)—it is wildly profitable.

In studying 4,658 actual business technology buyers, research organization Marketing Sherpa found that more than 50 percent admitted to short-listing a vendor after receiving a well-timed and relevant phone call.

In his very good book *Cold Calling for Chickens* (London: Cyan Communications), sales trainer Bob Etherington writes, "Fact: In any market 85 percent of the available new business goes to the 5 percent of sales people who know the secret of successful cold calling." Though Etherington uses the term *cold calling*, like most of those who teach the successful way to do it, the call is not that cold at all.

The same goes for another expert who has proven the effectiveness of prospecting, fellow author and sales consultant Paul DiModica. In his book, *Value-Added Selling*, he says,

> Cold Calling is the fastest way to increase your sales pipeline, your company's revenue, and your personal income. It is the difference between meeting a CFO of a *Fortune 500* company and selling to supervisors. If you were to analyze the top income sales positions in the U.S. (stockbrokers, commercial insurance salespeople, mergers and acquisitions salespeople) you would find that they all cold call.

Telephone prospecting is the quickest, cheapest, and most interactive way to make a contact and a sale. Consider this: Many of you reading this could pick up the phone right now, call someone you don't know and who never has heard of you, and have an electronic payment transaction minutes later.

Let's look at some of the other benefits of telephone prospecting:

You can enter a buying process that already is in progress. You may have been on the other end of this. Think of a situation where you were several calls, weeks, or months into a sales discussion with a prospect. Perhaps you were already well into the proposal phase. Then, suddenly, you are informed another competitor has entered the picture. What? You've done the tilling, planting, and nurturing, and they come later attempting to harvest the crop! Well, that's fair. But *you* want to be that guy, and prospecting does this for you.

Phone calling creates immediate opportunities for you that you never would have had previously. Hopefully, this does not come as a shock: Only a minuscule percentage of the world's population is looking for what you sell right now or is looking to buy from someone different. But a phone call can change all of that by bringing clients into a sales process immediately—even when they were not previously considering doing anything differently.

Calling creates future opportunities. To somewhat contradict the previous point, you can surely create immediate opportunities, but let's be realistic: Most of the people you call will not enter into an active sales cycle with you at that immediate moment. Some will simply and flat out *not* be prospects. However, there may be a *future* fit with others, even if the timing is not right today. Therefore, with regular prospecting, you methodically fill your pipeline with qualified prospects whom you subsequently enter into your automated stay-in-touch marketing campaign, so that when the time is right, you are top-of-mind.

It sharpens your sales skills. Anyone can react to an order or respond to a warm lead who contacts you. But the more you practice regularly—doing the right things—the better you become. Many salespeople left the profession over the past five years because it simply isn't as easy as it used to be. Good prospectors, however, are always in demand.

It's motivating! When you take action on anything and move toward a goal—especially if it is just a *bit* scary—it is impossible to feel down or depressed. Your mind becomes preoccupied with the task at hand, and you inherently find ways to accomplish it.

Cold Calling Myths, Smart Calling Truths

Before we go any further, I must dispel some prospecting myths that have been perpetuated over the years. Some of these beliefs are still held by sales managers and reps, and in all cases they are just plain wrong. They contribute to all of the negative opinions that surround telephone prospecting and general sales prospecting.

Cold Call Myth: "It's just a numbers game."

Smart Calling Truth: It's a *quality* game. It does not matter how many calls you place; what's important is the number with which you have success. A baseball player could swing at every pitch, but only the quality attempts have a chance of hitting the ball. Casino games are numbers games; sales and prospecting are a quality game.

Cold Call Myth: "For every no you get, you're that much closer to a yes."

Smart Calling Truth: You are no closer to a yes unless you are doing the right things to get the yes. The previous no has absolutely no bearing on your next call. Activity solely for the sake of activity does not get you closer to success.

Cold Call Myth: "You need to love rejection to be successful at prospecting."

Smart Calling Truth: You want to *avoid* rejection. It is a state of mind based on how you react to what happens to you. I'm not a psychologist, but I would say it is impossible to love rejection unless you have some type of mental illness. Smart Calling shows you how to get a win on every call—even when you get a no.

Cold Call Myth: "The telephone is just for setting an appointment."

Smart Calling Truth: Salespeople are using the telephone to sell every type of product and service. Limiting yourself by getting off a call too early unnecessarily lengthens the sales process. Your sales model might involve a face-to-face visit, but that visit will always be more productive if you take your call further.

Cold Call Myth: "Never give the screener any information."

Smart Calling Truth: The screener may be a decision maker or influencer and needs to be treated like the buyer. We will devote an entire section on this topic.

Still Think Prospecting Doesn't Work? That's News to Someone Doing It

Scott-Vincent Borba, CEO of BORBA (www.Borba.com), sells a line of high-end unique skin care products that are applied as well as ingested. In his first full year of business, Borba did $5 million in sales, and every deal he made started with a cold call. His products are carried by such companies as Saks, Sephora, Four Seasons Hotels, Victoria's Secret, and QVC.

In the early days, Borba made 60 prospecting calls a day. Although he is now, five years later, an established celebrity in the skin care field, he still makes prospecting calls. I asked what his revenue is today. He said his company is privately held, but revenues have increased 50 percent every year. I could do the math.

When I mentioned to him that there are people who believe that prospecting is dead and doesn't work, he screamed—even before I could ask a question—"That's crazy! Are you kidding me? I cold-called Anheuser-Busch and sold them on carrying my beauty water! These are beer guys!"

Borba has found such success in this area because he is prospecting the right way. He stresses the importance of knowing about the business issues of the company and the person he is calling. He also suggests that callers treat executive assistants like CEOs, since they are the decision makers' most trusted advisors. These people have often helped him get to and sell the C-level buyers with whom he works.

Any final words on successful prospecting from Borba?

"If you want something, you have to make it happen."

Okay, you might be thinking, *all of this makes sense*. Maybe you already knew you needed to pick up the phone to accomplish whatever objective you have to meet. The problems, though—the real reasons you bought this book—might still be gnawing at you: the *how?* part of it.

How can you make it more palatable to call someone you do not know?

How can you show success doing it?

How can you overcome the fear of the *no?*

How can you avoid using outdated, salesy techniques and sounding like the cheesy cold caller that everyone has experienced and has favorite horror stories about?

How can you avoid turning into a Jell-O-legged stutterer who sounds like a total doofus when confronted with the inevitable resistance?

The Answer: Smart Calling

The subtitle of this book is *Eliminate the Fear, Failure, and Rejection from Cold Calling*. I'm not being very humble when I claim that this is a great title that I'm proud to have created. However, it's not about me. It's about you and about how, together, we're going to do just what it promises.

Let's define in three steps exactly what Smart Calling is:

1. Acquiring intelligence about people, companies, and industries prior to speaking with a decision maker.

2. Using that information within a proven prospecting and sales process, speaking in a conversational, consultative dialogue that puts both you and the prospect at ease.

3. Consequently helping prospects take actions (buying from you) that they feel good about and from which they gain value.

As a result,

You get through to more buyers more often, since gatekeepers not only provide you with information but also become part of the process and your sales team.

Buyers are more receptive initially, in the first 10 to 20 seconds of the call—the time during which most calls fail.

Buyers don't view you as a typical salesperson or vendor but rather as someone who has their best interests in mind and can provide real value and return on investment.

You become more comfortable with your calls and confident in what you say—even in difficult situations.

You will never be rejected again. (You might be skeptical about this one, but you'll see exactly how and why this is the case later in the book.)

Smart Calling versus Cold Calling

Let's look at two sales calls from the same company.

One is a dumb call, very typical of what many salespeople do every day. Perhaps you have been there as well. The other will be the Smart Caller, who uses the process, strategy, and tactics we cover in this book.

Dumb Caller: "Hi, Mike, I'm Dale Dufus with Insurance Partners. We provide employee benefits, including health insurance. I'd like to take 10 minutes of your time and tell you what we do, and show you how we could save you time and money. I'll be in your area next week. Can we meet either Tuesday or Wednesday morning?"

In this brief, four-sentence opening, the caller made a number of dumb errors that would probably cause him to be rejected:

First, he assumed that the prospect went by a nickname and began by calling him "Mike." The list that Dale was working from had the contact name as Michael Jacobs, and Michael quickly corrected him. Ouch!

He merely stated what he sells: employee benefits and health insurance, with no explanation of value for Michael. There are hundreds of companies that sell the same thing, most of whom have already called Michael. People do not buy products or services *themselves*; they buy the result. Simply talking about products and services typically elicits a reaction of "We already have that" or "We are satisfied with what we have."

He wanted to *take* 10 minutes of Michael's time. Suggest to people that you want to *take* something of value from them without giving anything in return, and you immediately create resistance.

He was going to *tell* what he does, to which listeners instinctively react by thinking, *Here comes a sales pitch. I'm outta here!*

His only attempt at a value statement is the old, worn-out "save you time and money." This phrase is so overused and nondescript that it means nothing to most people.

Is Michael supposed to be excited that Dale will be in his area? Come on!

He asked for a decision: an appointment. Are you kidding? Michael does not see a reason to *stay on the phone* for another minute; he certainly would not waste time with a face-to-face meeting.

Now, let's look at a different sales professional from the same company, selling the same thing. His approach with Michael is quite different:

"Hi Michael, I'm Pat Stevens with Insurance Partners. Hope you enjoyed your golf vacation. In speaking with your assistant, Suzanne, I understand that you are in the process of evaluating your competitive edge in the employment market and what you can do to attract and keep the top talent in your various locations. We've been able to help other companies in the same situation lower their recruiting and hiring expenses, and increase their retention of managerial staff. I'd like to ask a few questions to see if I could provide you some information."

Using the Smart Calling strategy, process, and techniques, Pat was able to do a number of positive things:

> He used Michael's first name, since he knew that he was an informal guy and no one called him "Mr. Jacobs." However, he also knew that he hated to be called "Mike."
>
> He knew that Michael was a huge golf nut and had just returned from Arizona on a golf weekend with his buddies. He was able to mix in a little golf talk later in the call.
>
> He referenced Michael's assistant Suzanne, which gave credibility to the information he is relating.
>
> He knew that the company had recently lost some managerial candidates who were hired by the competition because of a better benefits package, as well as some existing employees who left the company for the same reason.
>
> He did not talk about insurance or benefits and instead discussed the *results* of doing business with his company—the precise results that addressed the issues that Michael now faced.

And all of that took place during the opening of the call—in the first 10 seconds or so. Later in the call—by using the Smart Calling process and techniques—Pat also:

> Asked questions to which he pretty much already knew the answers about the company's growth plans, their position in the marketplace, the existing benefits package, and how people felt about it.
>
> Commented on the great article that Michael had written for *Construction Executive* magazine.
>
> Asked about Michael's experience in working with one of his company's competitors prior to coming to work for this company two years ago.
>
> Joked that they both are lifelong Chicago Cubs fans who hope to see a championship yet in their lifetime.

As a result of all of this, Michael, of course, viewed Pat not as one of the hundreds of sales reps who call him every year schlepping insurance and benefits packages and offering quotes. He looked at Pat as someone who understood his business and what he was concerned about right now. Plus, he liked Pat. They connected.

But how did Pat accomplish all of this? How did he know all of these things? How did he speak in such a conversational way at the beginning of the call that captured Michael's interest? How did he avoid all of the dumb mistakes that typical salespeople commit?

Pat did his research before picking up the phone. He used several online resources to get personal and professional information about Michael, his company, his industry, and very importantly, what Michael was concerned about *right now*. Then Pat used social engineering, the process of speaking with other people within Michael's company to gain intelligence about the company's current situation regarding their recruiting, hiring, and retention issues and their present benefits package. He also learned about Michael personally from his assistant Suzanne and a few others in the department.

Pat used a conversational, soft-sell approach in his opening to minimize resistance, create interest, and pique curiosity. This put Michael in a state of mind where he wanted to hear more.

Pat used Smart Calling.

Now, don't get worried if what you sell might not require as much in-depth research as what Pat did. In some cases, just a little information is sufficient to turn your call into a Smart Call, and you will still benefit tremendously from this book. In summary, I can think of only two reasons why someone would opt *not* to place a Smart Call instead of a dumb cold call.

1. The sales rep is too lazy to put forth the effort.
2. The sales rep simply does not know what to do.

If you fall into that first category, I can't help you. In fact, you shouldn't even be in sales. However, if you are willing to work, then do not worry. I have the second reason covered for you. You are about to see exactly how to do it yourself. Hop aboard, my friend; here we go!

Pre-Call Planning

CHAPTER

2

Creating Your Possible Value Proposition

You will get whatever you want in life by helping enough others get what they want.

—Zig Ziglar

I often surprise the participants in my training workshops by spontaneously pulling out a digital camera and screaming, "Group photo time!" I tell them to smile, holler, and wave and that they can view the photo the next day on my Facebook fan page (www.Facebook.com/ ArtSobczak). Then I ask whose face they will look at first when they view the photo.

Of course, everyone sheepishly smiles and says, "Myself."

We then discuss how we all, mostly, care about ourselves. We're looking out for number one, baby.

But this might surprise some salespeople: Prospects do not share those same feelings about you. In fact, they do not care about you at all, because they have their own group photo mind-set. They are not concerned about your quota; they don't give a rat's behind about what you

21

want to do. You think you have a great product or service? Not a blip on their radar.

The prospects care mostly about . . . the prospects. About they will do next, and how it will affect them. And that is what *you* need to care mostly about as well: the prospect. If you want any chance at all at being successful with Smart Calling, everything you think about, do, and say needs to be about the prospect.

So get over yourself. You are not going to buy from you. From this point forward, it is all about *them*.

Where am I going with this?

When you embrace the all-about-them mind-set, you distinguish yourself from the typical self-interested salesperson or cold caller whom everyone tries to avoid. Two very basic fundamentals of sales that I have taught for more than 30 years are:

1. People love to buy but hate to be sold.
2. People buy for *their* reasons, not yours.

The all-about-them philosophy compels you to think about how to ideally build your calls using Smart Calling and allows us to do a couple of things in the process:

Understand the motivators of people who do and would buy from you.

Clearly articulate the possible value buyers may receive by buying from you.

This chapter's ultimate goal is for you to create Possible Value Propositions, which are the specific words and phrases you'll use in voice mails, with screeners, and in your opening statements. The statement's intent is to stimulate curiosity and interest in speaking with you while minimizing the chance for resistance. You also will use these Possible Value Propositions (PVPs) to develop need-uncovering questions to learn if your prospects see value in what you sell—or to help them see it.

As you make your way through this chapter, I'll insist that you do more than just read passively. You'll go through a series of exercises that require writing a number of statements and phrases that you'll plug into the Smart Call process later. *These exercises will provide the foundation for what you will say on your calls.* So go grab a pen and paper; I'll wait.

Understanding Your Prospects and Why They Might Buy from You

A major reason that so many new products fail is that companies create the product because *they* think it is a great idea. They do this instead of following the tried-and-true formula: Find a need and fill it.

Salespeople similarly fail because they try to sell what they think is cool, as opposed to understanding the prospects they are talking to and what they might want. To begin creating your Possible Value Propositions, we must first enter the worlds and minds of the people we call.

There was a very good show on NBC a few years ago called *Boomtown* that actually caused people to think. (That's probably why it got canceled after a season.) The show's premise was to examine one particular crime from a variety of viewpoints. For example, viewers might watch what appears to be a bank robber running from the scene of the crime. But as it turned out, when you heard the story told from the perspective of other people at the scene, various individuals had quite diverse slants on what actually occurred; even though they had all witnessed the same event.

What does this have to do with sales? As salespeople, *we* have opinions and feelings about why people should buy from us. However, our prospects might—and often do—have quite different thoughts and feelings. And again, what matters most? That's right: what *they* think.

You are not your customer. What you want, or the reasons you—or your marketing department—think someone should buy do not matter.

All right, I think you're ready now. Have that pen and paper? Let's get started with an exercise.

Picture all of the people involved in the decisions to buy or who influence the decision to buy what you sell. List them by what defines them. For example:

CEOs

Midlevel manager

Small business owner

Human resources recruiter

The person in charge of buying the copy paper in the office

Ask yourself the following questions and write out the answers for each person you've listed. (And don't freak out if you don't have all of the answers. As you talk to more prospects and customers, you'll have the opportunity to actually ask them and fill in any missing information.)

What Does Their Daily World Look Like?

Would a visit to your customers tell if they worked in a cubicle farm with hundreds of others or if they operate from whatever phone they pick up as they put out fires on the manufacturing floor? Is what you sell an integral component of their job, or is it just one of those tasks that needs to be done by *someone*, and they drew the short straw?

Putting yourself in someone else's shoes helps you better understand her thought processes—which enhances your ability to discern and discuss what may be of value to her.

How Are They Measured in Their Jobs? How Can You, and Your Products or Services, Possibly Impact That?

Appealing to buyers' personal needs is a secret of top sales reps—as well an often overlooked motivator. All clients have self-centered needs that they consider important within the scope of their jobs, needs that naturally affect their decisions. For example, they want to look good in their boss's eyes, they don't want to screw up the high-profile project their manager has given them, they need to hit their sales numbers so they get that bonus, they want to be respected among their industry peers, or they want to lessen their workload.

On the speaking and training side of my business, I'm often hired by meeting planners whose job it is to coordinate large national sales meetings for their clients—typically bigger companies. Of course, their professional objective is to pull off a successful event for their client. But I also know one of their personal motivators. After I had hit a home run with a workshop for a planner's client, she told me, "Wow, you made me look like a hero with them! They complimented me on hiring you." I could sense that having her ego stroked with such kudos had an impact on her beyond just the sense of a job well done. So now, when speaking with other meeting planners who are considering hiring me, I always ask, "What do you want your clients to tell you after a meeting?" Or "How can you look like a hero to your client after the meeting?" And I've even used it in voice mail messages and openings on Smart Calls: ". . . and other meeting planners have told me that our programs have helped them look like a hero in the eyes of their clients." (If you're in charge of hiring speakers/trainers for your firm/association, I can make you look like a hero, too: www.BusinessByPhone.com/hire-art/.)

What Do Buyers Typically Want as It Relates to Your Type of Products or Services?

Psychologists say that people are typically motivated by the desire to gain or by the fear of pain or loss. In this question—and the next one—we are applying these motivators to what we sell to help us understand what piques people's interest. So, be specific when you answer. Get sensory with your descriptions. For example, a software sales rep should not say, "Clients want good customer service." That's vague. A better answer is "Users want their technical support calls answered the first time they call, without being put on hold or having to leave a message." That's easier to visualize, isn't it? It stirs more emotion, which is what we want to do to get people to move in our direction.

Other examples include:

Increased targeted web traffic, resulting in more click-throughs and sales.

Larger average sales on inbound calls.

More productivity per hour on the assembly line.

A higher customer satisfaction rating from their buyers.

Right now, brainstorm and write out your own buyer wants. Put yourself in your buyers' position, and figure out exactly what *their* end goal would be.

What Do Buyers Typically Want to Avoid as It Relates to Your Type of Products or Services?

This is where you define the pain factor. Social scientists tell us that people will do more to avoid pain than they will do to gain pleasure, so this could provide even stronger Possible Value Propositions for you. Here are just a few examples of how Smart Callers could help their prospects avoid pain:

Avoid costly lawsuits.

Avoid fines because of noncompliance with state regulations.

Minimize turnover in the call center.

Eliminate duplication of data entry.

Lower the cost of virtually anything (more on this one later).

You've probably noticed that just thinking about and writing down your answers gets you further inside your prospects' minds and allows you to better understand their perspectives and ways of thinking—the ideal spot from which to prepare for and execute your Smart Calls.

The other benefit is that you have just crafted word-for-word phrases that you may be able to polish and plug into your voice mails and interest-generating openings. Congratulations—you have begun building your Possible Value Propositions! Let's dig deeper into what these are and explore more ways to help define yours.

Defining Your Possible Value Propositions

You've probably noticed that I've used the term *Possible* Value Proposition several times. What's up with the "possible" part, you may be wondering? Well, if you've been through any type of sales training, you may have been taught to sell the benefits. But there are some problems with that.

Most of what sales reps and marketing people *believe* to be benefits are actually not at all of personal interest to prospects. These benefits simply state facts about products and services and are many times just cutesy slogans that mean nothing.

A benefit is of value only if the person hearing it perceives it to be of value *at that very moment*. What is beneficial to someone today may be meaningless a few months from now.

Value is not what *you* say it is; it is always what the buyer perceives it to be.

Most important (this should be blown up in big letters and put on a poster in your office), buyers perceive value as a *result* of owning and using your product or service. The value is in the outcome—not the product or service itself. They become interested and buy because they see a photo of the end result, with themselves in the picture.

This is why I call it your *Possible* Value Proposition. There are other authors, trainers, and gurus who term these your unique value proposition or simply your value prop. However, I think it's important to remember that everything we create and believe to be of value for our prospects is just that: what *we* think it is. And it remains this way until we find out for certain, by talking to our prospects, asking questions, listening to the answers, and then digging deeper.

Oh sure, these things have been of great value for others; they may be for *most* prospects and probably will be for our prospects. We'll just need to confirm that on our calls. Using the term *possible* helps us not be too presumptuous, which could cause us to pitch something without asking questions first.

So—keeping all of this in mind—we'll now examine what to avoid and then what to do when creating your Possible Value Propositions.

What to Avoid (or Things That Would Cause Your Prospect to Say, "So What?")

I was in my car, stopped at a traffic light, when I glanced at the pickup truck next to me. It was a typical construction work vehicle. Underneath the company name, in big letters, was its motto:

Practically Perfect Vinyl Siding

Huh? I did a double take.

Would I want siding that was just *practically* perfect? Is there a discount if it's just practically perfect?

I understand that maybe if you give this some thought—perhaps even referencing your *Webster's*—you could argue that they have another intended meaning for "practically perfect." But the first impression that entered my mind was that it did nothing for me. In fact, it was negative.

Too often, I run into companies whose sales reps are told to use phrases on their calls that were drafted by an advertising copywriter who has never sold anything. Sometimes they are just repeating a company motto, like *We Unfold the Technology of Tomorrow, Today.*

What? What on earth does that mean?

We've Been in Business for Over____Years. Or We're the Largest . . .

And that helps me . . . how?

We're the Most Experienced in the Industry

According to what criteria, and how does that affect me?

We're the Most Respected . . .

Oh, really, by whom? That's as meaningless as when CNN says it's the most respected name in news.

We're a National Company with 30 Locations

What if I'm a little company doing business in my local zip code? A training client in the banking supply business shared how he was telling a prospect that he sold to such big banks as Chase, Bank of America, and CitiBank. The prospect, unimpressed, replied, "Oh. You're too big for us then. We're just a local community bank, and I don't think we'd get the service we want."

We Have a Commitment to Quality

That's nice. Who doesn't? How will that help me, specifically?

We Were the First to . . .

So? What have you done since then, and how will it help me?

We Provide Cost-Effective Solutions . . .

Uh-huh, and that means . . . what, . . . exactly, as it relates to what I want?

And just because something is free does not make it a benefit, either. A guy working the US Airways MasterCard booth at the Phoenix airport was standing in the middle of the concourse yelling to anyone who would listen, "Free stuff!" He apparently was giving away some type of T-shirt or stuffed animal in exchange for signing up for the credit card. I wasn't quite sure, though, since I, like everyone else, went out of my way to *avoid* him and not make eye contact. The free item was not a benefit because I already had the card.

I heard a radio commercial the other day that offered a special report on preventing some physical malady and at the end implored, "Call right now! The phone call is *free!*" You could have offered to *pay* me to call, but I wouldn't have; I wasn't interested in the report.

What's my point? Free is not a benefit in and of itself, but countless salespeople seem to think it is, and they use it to try to create interest. For example, "Hi, Mr. Prospect, I'm with Network Security Associates, and I'd like to offer you a free network security evaluation." If the product, service, or thing that is the main deliverable is not desirable, it doesn't matter if it is free.

The purpose of providing you with all of these examples is that we must clearly state some possible value for our prospects. It must answer their question: "What does this do for me?" Let's continue and explore more ways to create your PVP.

Pain and Gain

You made a list earlier of what your prospective buyers want and what they want to avoid, relating to your type of product or service. (You *did* do that, didn't you? Go back if you haven't—this is important stuff.)

Look at those answers again. Hopefully, you and your product or service can deliver much—or all—of what you wrote regarding what prospects want and don't want. Those are Possible Value Propositions.

You can also combine the pain and gain into one PVP. For example, a sales rep for a construction contractor could say, *"We specialize in working with landlords whose properties failed building inspections and fix them so they pass."*

Here are some additional ideas for identifying more PVPs.

The Easy Way to Provide Possible Value

The radio commercial claimed, *"Lose weight the easy way. No more sweaty gyms. No more starving yourself. No exercise. Simply take this pill . . ."*

Yeah, right. The sad thing is that their phones probably went crazy with orders. People like to do things the easy way whenever they can.

Just notice some of the other ads that are always on TV: one wrench that does the job of an entire clumsy toolbox of them, little pads to place under your furniture and appliances so you can move them with little effort, a vegetable chopper that takes a fraction of the time of chopping with a knife, and so on.

Your e-mail inbox today probably has some pitches with this theme: Get rich quick by doing nothing more than reading e-mail, and make money in your jammies.

And who doesn't want the easier way? Office supply company Staples has run a very successful ad campaign around the Easy Button. We all wish we had one; the reasons aren't always the same, though. Some people are lazy. Others, however, are so motivated, busy, and overworked that simplifying some tasks will free up more time for others. Most people are somewhere in between. Whatever the case, ease is a universally attractive benefit.

Is this something you can provide? If so, define how. Fill in the following blanks:

We make it easier for companies/individuals to _____.

We cut down the amount of time it takes to _____.

We help eliminate the dreaded tasks of _____.

We cut down on the hassle of _____.

We lessen the stress of _____.

Are You Able to Help Cut Costs?

Cutting costs is usually a strong Possible Value Proposition, since it is one way for a company to increase profits. Is this something you can affect? How do you help companies or individuals control or cut costs?

Think of how you can use any of these phrases to describe the results you provide your prospects and customers.

Cut the costs of . . .

Reduce expenses on . . .

Trim the fat from . . .

Lower the payments on . . .

Lessen the . . .

Control the costs of . . .

Reduce interest rates on . . .

Eliminate the waste in . . .

Minimize the number of . . .

Prevent increases in . . .

Pay less for . . .

Get discounts on . . .

Increase the amount of _____ they get, for the same price they're paying now

Find the best prices for . . .

Reduce spending on . . .

Delay increases in . . .

Consolidate the bills for . . .

Take advantage of credits for . . .

Reduce debt . . .

How Are You Different?

Another way to strengthen your Possible Value Proposition is to separate yourself from the masses. Be different. Kind of like the Two Hip Chicks.

Let me explain.

While driving into my suburban neighborhood, I paid little attention to the collection of hand-drawn and Home Depot–purchased signs cluttering the street corner, all of which screamed out: GARAGE SALE! However, one grabbed my eye:

Two Hip Chicks Garage Sale

Selling Our Cool Stuff

Now, I'm not a rummage sale kind of guy; but I went out of my way and turned down the street to see what this was all about. Not sure of what to expect, I drove by the house. It pretty much looked the same as the other garage sales I passed along the way, with one exception:

There were *lots* of people at this one.

That didn't surprise me.

The Hip Chicks set themselves apart from the masses. They added a little emotion and psychology to the mix. After all, who wouldn't want used stuff that is hip and cool, as opposed to someone's junk that will be thrown away if they don't sell it?

So, what makes *you* different? What sets you and your company apart? What are the advantages you have over your competition?

Let's face it: Lots of companies sell exactly the same thing. Yet some manage to thrive while others struggle or go out of business. The difference maker is—well, the difference.

If you think you can't do this because you feel you sell a commodity, you are probably right. Your cause will be hopeless. That's because *you* must first believe in the difference that you offer, whether it's price, quality, or service.

If we can differentiate a dead chicken, you can differentiate anything.
                              —Frank Perdue, founder of Perdue Farms

I heard a great differential advantage on a radio commercial: *"There are lots of services you could pick from, but at One-Hour Heating and Air, if we're not on time, you don't pay a dime."*

I thought Walmart's old value statement, "Always Low Prices. Always," was better than the new one: "Save Money. Live Better." They never asked me.

There's a local computer company that runs a great ad differentiating itself from the chain electronics retailers by making fun of how technical and impersonal the big-box boys are with customers. Their ads end with this differentiating line: *"Bottom line, we will be cheaper, faster, and more polite than the computer chain stores."*

Here's an example of a sales rep trying to create value: *"Hi, Ms. Prospect, I'm Joe Seller with Contractor's Supply. We sell drywall supplies, and I'd like to tell you what we sell and see if we could become one of your suppliers."*

Yawn. He's basically saying that he does the same thing as every other drywall supplier. Worse, his comments are likely to incite resistance, since he's suggesting that he wants to sell something.

Here's a much better version that differentiates the caller:

Hi, Ms. Prospect, I'm Joe Seller with Contractor's Supply. In talking with Jean in your office, I understand that your installers now spend quite a bit of time leaving jobs and running to your supplier to pick up materials when they need something. What sets us apart is that we have trucks out that offer delivery within an hour when contractors need something. I'd like to ask a few questions to see if what we offer might be of value to you.

That was a Possible Value Statement actually plugged into the interest-creating opening. We will cover how to do that in depth later.

Here are a couple of others:

Jane, I'm Pat Sellar with Info Industries. Like many people who are probably now calling you, I saw the news about how your network was compromised by a cyberattack. We specialize in helping companies protect their customer information from theft or viral attack, and what sets us apart is . . .

Allison, I'm A. J. Scott with Murano Consulting. My compliments on your recent article about the state of the recruiting business. We have worked with a number of search firms in helping their recruiters cut down on the number of days it takes to fill their positions. I know you might get a lot of calls like this as a result of the article, but what we do differently is . . .

Now it's time for you to define your own differential advantages. Brainstorm and simply fill in the blanks:

What sets us apart is _____.

What makes us different is _____.

Something that you'll get from us that no one else offers is _____.

The Value You Have Already Provided for Others

Some of your strongest, most interesting, and impactful PVPs will simply describe what you have already done for your other customers. These are the specific results your customers have realized.

For the following exercise, I want you to research your 20 biggest sales. Also include the customers who have been buying from you the longest. You are looking for the answers to this simple question: What specific, tangible, and measurable results did they realize by being your customer?

This will provide you with more Possible Value Propositions. For example:

We have helped other pediatric dentists cut their cost of new patient acquisition by an average of 50 percent, while increasing their number of new patients by 25 percent within six months.

We've allowed publishing clients that were using 5 to 10 different programs to manage the various aspects of their online marketing and sales to replace all of their programs with just one, cutting their software costs, saving hours of time, and in some cases, doubling their print and ebook sales.

Recruiters who use our career postings tell us that the candidates they attract are better qualified, meaning they save hours per week by not having to deal with applicants who would never be considered.

Now I know there are some people reading this—not you, of course—who aren't quite sure why people bought from them, or what the results were afterward. Not a problem—just ask them. Call your customers and say, "Pam, we appreciate your business and want to be sure that we continue to give you everything you want and expect from us. To that end, I'd like to ask a few questions. Please tell me, what were some of the main reasons you bought from us initially? And what specific results have you received from working with us?"

Listen to their responses, and then dig deeper. Prompt them to attach numbers to their answers. Get dollar amounts: The more specific the information, the better.

In her e-book *Developing Strong Value Propositions*, author Jill Konrath, who helps sales pros sell to big companies, said, "I had lunch with the president of a half-billion-dollar division of a major corporation. She told me that if someone contacted her and said he could reduce waste by just 1 percent, she would meet with him immediately. Why? Because she knew exactly how much her company spent on waste—and it was a lot of money. Every penny she saved would go right to the bottom line."

I recommend that you get a copy of Jill's free e-book. It's one of the best, most comprehensive resources I've seen on coming up with value propositions. You can download it at www.jillkonrath.com/value-proposition-kit/ and get a few other valuable goodies.

Smart Calling Tip

When customers volunteer a positive statement about any result they have experienced by buying from you in a normal conversation, ask them if you could use that when you speak with other prospective customers. Tell them you will put it in an e-mail and request that they reply to give their approval. Then set up a "Testimonial/PVP" folder in your e-mail program or customer relationship management (CRM) system.

Do You Help Inadequacy?

Here's an especially powerful possible buying motivator: *inadequacy*.

Think about all the ads out there for products and services that help with conditions like hair loss, being overweight, body parts too large or too small, and personal appearance deficiencies of any other type. One of the longest-running magazine classified ads is for shoe lifts to make men taller.

Does your product or service affect inadequacy in any way? For example—and recalling what we covered earlier about helping your buyers *personally*—can you help any of your buyers improve their status within their company or industry? Are they fed up with getting smacked around by the competition and losing out when they reply to requests for proposals? Do their products get negative reviews in the online forums?

I often hear from managers whose sales reps are fearful of picking up the phone to prospect. When they finally do call, they lack confidence and consequently get blown off their calls—setting off the chain reaction of poor morale and call avoidance. One of my PVPs is "*I have helped sales reps who previously were uncomfortable with and lacked confidence in prospecting to actually enjoy the process, and double their number of new accounts.*"

Define if and how inadequacy might be felt by your buyers—and let them know exactly how the results of your product or service can fix it.

Value Is Not the Same for Everyone

A final thought on understanding your prospects and defining value: Even though they may be employed by the same company, everyone involved in your buying process probably does not define value in the same way.

If you were at a party, for instance, would you talk to the third-grade daughter of the host the same way you would speak with a college professor in attendance? Of course not! So let's put this in perspective: Do you sell the same way to the different types of buyers of your products or services? If so, that's like sending an identical direct mail piece to every prospect, hoping it touches on something they all are interested in.

A purchasing agent has dissimilar needs from a product or service user. A twenty-something MBA fastracking to his next promotion views purchases differently than a fiftyish middle manager going through the motions, avoiding risks, and flying under the radar until retirement. The guy who maintains the grass outside the office has a different perspective from the person looking out at it from her top-floor corner office.

Again, the key element is what you think about before your call. Clearly, if you're only thinking *sell*, you're sorely misguided. The correct mind-set is *Who am I talking to, and what might they want?*

As you identify the different levels within an organization you might speak with—or at least those who are affected by what you sell—be sure you have clarified the PVPs for each. For example:

Executive Assistants. They want to know: "Does this sound like a self-interested time-wasting salesperson, or someone who might have something worth my boss's time?"

Users of Your Product or Service. They are interested in how they will be affected, directly and otherwise. Will you make their job more difficult and cause them more short- and long-term work, or will you have the opposite effect? They're interested in the technical, how-to aspects. (*Important point*: At this level and lower, a solution that could help eliminate waste and labor duplication might also serve to eliminate their jobs or those of their friends, so be cognizant of what you are suggesting.)

Managers of the Users of Your Product or Service. How will you affect their overall department? They are similar to the users but also concerned about how it will fit within a budget.

Top-Level Executives. They aren't as concerned about the details as they are about the end result you can deliver, particularly for the long term. Usually, it is the return on investment.

You have now worked to define what possible value you might be able to provide for your prospects, and you are in a *Them* frame of mind. We now will work on making our calls Smart.

Smart Calling Action Steps

What else will you commit to *do* as a result of this chapter?

Intelligence Gathering

Making Your Calls Smart

Prepare to win, or lose to someone who is.

—Jeffrey Gitomer

What differentiates a dumb cold call from a Smart Call is, first, what you learn about a prospect and his situation. We can modify the old saying, "It's all about who you know" to "It's all about WHAT you know, about who you want to know, in order to actually get to know them."

But it's not just about information. Perhaps you've heard the quote attributed to Sir Francis Bacon: "Knowledge is power." However, with respect to Sir Francis, knowledge is *not* power. To quote Calvin Coolidge, "There are lots of educated derelicts."

The power comes in how you *use* this knowledge, which we will discuss later in the book. In this chapter, we'll cover intelligence gathering: what you want to learn and, then, where to find it.

What Information Do You Want about Your Prospects?

The intelligence you seek depends on what you sell and why someone would buy. Simpler sales—those that are more transactional and have a shorter sales cycle, such as an ad in the community magazine—are not likely to warrant as much time as a seven-figure sale for consulting services to a *Fortune 100* company. However, the same processes and techniques can be used in both situations.

In general, you are looking for factual data as well as situational information. Facts include basic statistics, such as how many locations or number of employees the company has, their financial results, and, as obvious as this might seem, what the company actually *does*. However, I'm not shy to repeat what should be obvious since I know most people—including myself—regularly need to be reminded of the fundamentals.

As an example, it boggles my mind how salespeople can pick up the phone to call a company without even knowing what they sell. For example, my company's name is Business By Phone Inc. I am regularly prospected by clueless callers who think that we are a phone system reseller, an outsourced call center, or a company much larger than we are, since they pitch me on services appropriate only for companies with more than 50 employees. Dumb.

Beyond acquiring the basic facts, the real jackpot lies within the situational information you uncover. This is anything about the company, industry, or individual that may make them a good prospect for you because of a need, pain, problem, desire, or other circumstance on their part. For example:

- A bank is building two new branch locations.
- A furniture company is being sued because of alleged faulty construction in one of its products.
- A manager at any company has just been promoted to VP.
- A CEO is interviewed by a blog author about trends in his industry and shares some initiatives they are working on this year.
- According to a national study, demand is sizzling for locally grown organic food items in grocery stores
- New state regulations require small service businesses to collect and report sales taxes where they did not before.

Think big picture for a moment about the chains of events that could create needs, pains, problems, and desires for the people and companies involved in those situations. Consequently, there are countless opportunities for all kinds of businesses that help solve those problems or fulfill those desires. Construction companies, law firms, recruiters, anyone who helps increase sales, software developers and installers—the list is endless.

Here are a few other activities that could create an environment in which someone would be eager to hear about an appropriate Possible Value Proposition:

- Awarding of contracts.
- Expansion or downsizing—geographically, personnel-wise, divisions or subsidiaries, product or service offerings.
- Legal actions initiated, or the target thereof.
- Restructuring.
- Initiatives of any type: cost-cutting, pushing for more sales, becoming more customer-focused, streamlining network operations, getting a greater return on investment (ROI) on anything.
- Change of most types: new personnel, products, or product introductions.
- Any other compelling event, such as a new product launch or deadlines of any type.

Identify and Look for Trigger Events

Craig Elias was a top sales rep for telecommunications company World-Com. During its collapse, Craig realized that he could either find another company to sell for or do something on his own. He chose the latter. He felt that he could help other sales reps use a model he discovered and fine-tuned while rising to the top at Worldcom.

When analyzing his six- and seven-figure sales, he noticed a trend emerging. Every sale was a result of a trigger event that shifted a prospect from being someone who never would have bought from him previously into someone who was highly likely to buy from him now. These events moved people into what Elias calls the window of dissatisfaction. Elias's model identifies three categories of trigger events. Determine how they apply to your buyers:

1. *Bad Experience:* The buyer has an unpleasant experience with people, a product or service, or a provider. For instance, there may have been

a product or service change with their existing supplier that creates dissatisfaction.

2. *Change or Transition:* The buyer has a change or transition in people, places, or priorities. For instance, there may have been a change in the buyer at an account.

3. *Awareness:* The buyer becomes aware of the need to change for legal, risk-avoidance, or economic reasons. For instance, the person may have a new understanding that buying from someone like you is less risky or cheaper than continuing to buy the existing solution.

These events are the types of information you would like to learn before speaking with your decision maker.

Craig has a useful free tool at his site called a "Won Sales Analysis" that I suggest you download. Instead of focusing on the sales you've lost, this application helps you analyze the sales you've *won* to help identify the common trigger events that place buyers in that window of dissatisfaction. Get it at www.WonSalesAnalysis.com. (Also, get a copy of his fine book *SHiFT! Harness the Trigger Events That Turn Prospects Into Customers.*)

I actually experienced a trigger event while working on this chapter. I had taken a couple of full days to do nothing but write while at my Arizona home. I'm diligent about regularly saving my work as I write—especially something this lengthy and important. When it came time for me to leave for my other office at the time, in Omaha, I went to e-mail myself the two chapters I had written so that I would have them on my main office machine. However, they were nowhere to be found! I'm no tech novice, and I just knew they had to be hiding *somewhere.* I frantically searched for the files. Nada. Talk about a sick feeling! To make things worse, my flight was leaving in 90 minutes. Wanting to continue my search, I quickly added the GoToMyPC service to that computer, since I could then access it from any Internet-connected computer later. (I never did locate the files. Luckily, I had printed out hard copies and was able to re-create them—with some pain and expense.)

Now, I would imagine that at Citrix, the GoToMyPC people, their sales reps—if they practice a form of Smart Calling—would want to know if prospects and their employees ever work from home or another remote location and whether they ever had emergency situations where they needed to search for data on another machine. (This is something you can learn by doing social engineering, which we will cover shortly.)

Smart Calling Exercise

1. List the factual information you would like to learn about your prospects before a call.
2. Identify the situational information you would like to learn prior to your calls.

Getting Personal

In addition to acquiring information on the company, it's helpful to be knowledgeable about the people. What information is important to know? Whatever is available. Dig for what you can find out about them personally and in their professional lives. I'm by no means suggesting you mention or *use* everything you learn, since you don't want to come across as a creepy stalker. A female client told me a sales rep cold-called her and, in the opening, told her that he saw her picture online and liked her smile. (I can hear the collective "Ewwwww!") You, of course, need to be judicious and use the information appropriately.

This becomes valuable when you can make a closer connection with your prospect by asking questions later in a call (questions you will probably know the answer to: "I'm assuming you're an LSU football fan?") or making a comment about what you know: "By the way, I always like to be prepared for my calls and did some research. That was a great article you wrote for the Components Insight website."

In his classic book *Swim with the Sharks (without Being Eaten Alive)*, author Harvey Mackay explained the tool he required his sales reps to use, called the Mackay 66. It is 66 pieces of information that reps need to collect about their prospects and customers: business background, special interests, their lifestyle, business needs, and the nature of the rep's relationship with them. (Although it was written in the mid-1980s, the book is still relevant, and I recommend it. If you would like to see the Mackay 66 right now, go to www.harveymackay.com/pdfs/mackay66.pdf.)

He Won This Sale

An item in the *Wall Street Journal* nicely illustrated the power of getting—and using—information about those with whom you will soon be meeting or working. A headhunter interviewing for his own new job came armed with files on 10 people within the firm (from the CEO on down) that he'd ideally like to meet with. When he spoke with his interviewers, they saw his categorized notebook, stuffed with notes and web pages on the individuals. This, of course, impressed them, since he had clearly done his homework, and he was offered a job as a partner at the firm.

And this book resulted in at least one similar story:

Sales pro David Flannery wrote,

> I ordered your book to help me get a $100,000 Business Development Manager position. The final interview test was to make a sales call to the company CEO, and sell him his own company. I used everything you taught in the book . . . and GOT THE JOB. During the de-brief the following day, I asked "What specifically got me the position?" Every single point brought up by the CEO were things I learned in your book. I want to thank you so much!

Where to Find Your Smart Information

Although I certainly don't *feel* like I'm in my early fifties—and friends say I still think and act like a juvenile fairly often—I can sound like a crotchety old fogy when I'm talking about the environment we sell in today. I often feel like saying, "When I was your age, youngster, we weren't able to go click, click, click and have almost everything we want to know about a prospect appear on this TV screen in front of us before we call him."

Today's technology makes it quick and easy to acquire valuable information that can Smarten up your calls. In fact, there is *no excuse* for *not* having information about your prospects before you call. The only argument I've heard otherwise—which I still don't buy–is that reps can't afford to take the time before a call to do research. They claim that they need to be on the phone, constantly placing calls, and can't occupy themselves with research. Bull! That's the numbers game mentality of throwing it all up against the wall and seeing what sticks. I can't think of any situation— even the simplest, most basic transactional call—that wouldn't yield better results and be worth the time invested to know something about the person and company.

Another thing: How many attempts, on average, does it take before you actually get someone live on the phone? The numbers vary wildly, but the point is that you are not doing all of that research before each attempt.

You do the bulk of it once, you make the attempt, you put the relevant information in your Customer Relationship Management (CRM) system, then you remind yourself of it prior to your next attempt.

So let's explore where we can find this kind of information.

Your Database

Talk about another one of those "Well, duh, no kidding" points. *Of course*, you should check your company's database before calling a prospect to see if there is any history there. But again, the obvious isn't always followed. I have personally heard many calls where salespeople prospected individuals they *thought* were prospects—only to hear, "Are you kidding me? We've been buying from you for years!" Oops. Now *that's* embarrassing.

So always check the notes for any comments from previous contacts, if any, and certainly look to see if there were any past purchases.

Smart Calling Tip

Past customers are one of your best sources of new business. There is *gold* in this list. And don't be afraid if the customer quit buying because of a problem. The problem will still exist—or at least be remembered—if no one bothers to contact them. However, calling will give you a chance to fix it. And if the previous buyer left, go through the Smart Calling process with the new buyer. You can always reference the previous relationship, and you have some history to work with.

Exploring the Wealth of Online Information

Your Prospect's Website

Your prospect's website should be your first online destination. Again, what you sell will determine where you drill, but aside from the obvious facts you would find at their site, here are a few other ideas about specific places to go:

> **The "About Us" Section.** This is often where you'll be able to find names, bios, and contact info for key people, as well as details on how the company began, who they serve, what benefits

or tools they provide, and perhaps who some of their major clients are.

Press Releases. These provide timely information that the company obviously believes is newsworthy, as well as potential contact names when you're otherwise coming up empty. Heather Beck, a sales rep with testing equipment manufacturer Acterna, said that she was more than once unable to get a contact name from an operator or anywhere on a website but found someone quoted in a press release that she could then call. Though this person wasn't the buyer, speaking with him gave her a start with some names in the investigation and navigation process.

Mission Statements. Ryzex Group manager Peter Andrachuk suggests looking for key words and phrases that signify importance to the company. For example, evaluate the company's mission statement or simply the description on their home page of what they do. If they say that one of their goals is to "make the lives of their customers easier through automation of daily, routine tasks," then that could be a phrase you could use in a letter, e-mail, voice mail, and opening statement.

Job Postings. These could indicate situational change, such as expansion, and certainly personnel change (new people in new roles—perhaps that of the buyer). A sales rep for phone equipment told me he would call into the department that handled the company's telecommunications and discuss the upcoming needs they might have with the additional employees. In addition to checking a company's site for postings, check www.Indeed.com, a compilation site for online job postings.

Company Site Searches. Some company websites have a search box that makes it much easier to hunt for specific information within the site. Here's a way to do it using Google: Type your search term in quotes, then site:companysite.com. For example, if I am looking for sales managers at Verizon, I would search "sales manager" site:verizon.com.

Guessing E-mail Addresses. If you know a company's e-mail address protocol, you can likely guess addresses if you know names. For example, if on a press release I see that the PR manager's name is Pamela Dennard, and her e-mail is PDennard@ABCorp.com, then I have a fairly good idea what Jerry Noble's e-mail will be at the same company.

Smart Call Success Story: How a Rep Gathers and Uses Intelligence from a Prospect's Site

A regional account manager with McGraw-Hill Construction Dodge, Tim Nelson says, "I think the most important [thing] I learn from [an organization's] website is how the company portrays itself. I sell new project information to architects, engineers and general contractors, and they all have 'brag sites' that tell of the jobs they've built. That tells me their focus. It also gives me an indication of their [level of] Internet savvy-ness, as this will affect how someone would use our solution.

"Their sites also [let me know] who the principals and heads of other offices are that might be impacted by the information I sell. Knowing about other key people allows me to be more pointed in my questioning. Instead of asking 'Does anyone else need to be involved with this?' I can say, 'Since this will also impact your Project Management team, does Doug need to be involved in any of this?'"

Other Online Resources

There are numerous places you can go to gather intelligence online, several of which I'll mention. However, I could just skip my entire discussion on using the Internet to gather information and defer to Sam Richter, whose life's work is devoted to just that. Sam's book *must* be a part of your library if you are serious about prospecting. It's *Take the Cold Out of Cold Calling— Web Search Secrets: Know More than You Ever Thought You Could (or Should) about Your Prospects, Clients, and Competition* (www.TakeTheCold.com).

Sam is an expert at finding information about people, companies, and industries online, and his book provides advanced tips for using search engines as well numerous sites to visit to collect intelligence. There's information available online that you probably never thought was accessible. Sam and I have done a number of seminars and webinars together, and what he teaches is must-have information for Smart Callers.

I of course won't try to paraphrase his entire book, but here's just a taste of just a couple of the techniques Richter presents for using Google.

"Filetype" Searches. You can type a company name in quotes and then filetype:, followed by a file extension to locate online files publicly available. For example, if you're looking for white papers a company had posted on its site, you would type "Johnson Engi-neering" filetype:pdf. This can be done for all types of files, such as PowerPoints, spreadsheets, and documents. (Sam also cautions that it may not be ethical to use everything you find because it is possible to locate files that a company did not realize were actu-ally posted at its site.)

Street View. Depending on what you sell, it could be useful for you to see an actual photo of your prospect's location. Click on "Maps" at the top of the Google home page, and enter the street address. Then you can use the various tools to move the photo around and zoom in.

I wish I was getting a commission on my recommendation for this book, but I'm not. If you are serious about Smart Calling, though, you absolutely need it. It's under $25. Trust me on this; get it. Sam's site (www. TakeTheCold.com) also has other free resources for you that can Smarten your calls, including a free toolbar.

Smart Calling Search Tip

Geographic software company LizardTech's John Ruffing shared an interesting idea about finding people who are buying. If you sell to gov-ernments at any level, do Internet searches for "Requests for Proposal" and your key words. He said that most government entities must post their RFPs, and this is therefore a good way to find them.

Google News Alerts

Google News Alerts (http://www.google.com/alerts) is a free service that needs to become part of your Smart Calling toolbox. Google will send you e-mail at the frequency of your choice (even daily) that notifies you of any new content posted to the web containing the search term(s) that you determine. At minimum, you should have alerts set up with your main competitors' names and those of your biggest customers. You should also include both the company name and the names of individual decision mak-ers of your most highly coveted prospects. You can enter queries for what-ever you'd like, including specific terms such as "building permits in 68137 zip code." Google is your part-time lead generator, and works for free!

How to Steal Business When Your Competitor Undergoes Changes

Here's how to use a Google News Alert to be notified of what could be a trigger event for you: A friend told me how his business bank recently changed owners and names . . . *three times*. One astute bank sales rep who has been pursuing him manages to contact him after each change while the effects are fresh in his mind. Although he hasn't moved yet, the timely calls combined with the annoyance of the changes are beginning to wear down his resistance.

Change is inevitable; it happens every day. And Smart sales reps have processes in place to take advantage of change. A couple of sales points for you:

- Prospects can be particularly vulnerable after their existing vendor is acquired, is merged, or undergoes some other type of change.
- Capitalizing on this change requires that you track from whom a prospect buys, monitor any changes, and then be able to sort your database accordingly and place an effective call.

So here's *exactly* what to do:

1. Set up a Google News Alert with the names of your top competitors. When anything happens with them that appears online, you will be notified based on the key words you enter.
2. Set up a Current Vendor field or group that is searchable in your CRM system or contact management program. Find out on every future Smart Call with new prospects which vendor they are buying from (which could be a secondary objective; see how all of this falls into place?). Then, it's a breeze to do a quick sort of all the prospects who have the competitor's name in the field and plan strategically timed contacts when changes make it appropriate.
3. Call with value. Naturally, you don't phone these prospects exuding an attitude of "So I see your vendor was just acquired. I bet things are a mess there! Why don't you switch to us?" Instead, pique some interest in the opening by hinting at value, and be prepared to ask questions designed to get them to tell you the problems and pains they may be experiencing as a result of the change. For example:

"Mike, I had called you six months ago, and we discussed how I might be able to help cut some of your component costs. At the time you mentioned you were with AB Vending, and a change at that point didn't seem too timely. With the recent acquisition of AB, some of my other customers have noticed some changes in the promptness of getting orders delivered. If that is an issue for you, we have some options that might be worth taking a look at . . ."

Again, be sure that prospects don't view your opening as the just-checking-in-with-you type of call or a call that falls into one of the many categories of mistakes reps often make with their openings. (You can find more on the mistakes—and what to do instead—in the opening statement chapters.)

LinkedIn

In the first edition of this book I strongly recommended you use LinkedIn. Now I absolutely insist on it. If you are serious about Smart Calling, LinkedIn is the professional network for businesspeople. Period.

On the surface, LinkedIn can be described as a social network for business, where users post their professional information and experience and also can connect with others. In reality, it is a sophisticated tool that offers many layers of potentially valuable services to help you Smarten your calls, get into more sales conversations, and close more business.

I will not claim to be an expert on LinkedIn, although there are many around. I suggest you learn from them. There are hundreds of articles on how to prospect and sell using the service. A search on Amazon.com for "LinkedIn" brought over 1,500 book titles. One that I particularly like is *Maximizing LinkedIn for Sales and Social Media Marketing: An Unofficial, Practical Guide to Selling & Developing B2B Business on LinkedIn* by Neal Schaffer. His website is http://windmillnetworking.com, where he has updated blog posts not only on LinkedIn, but other areas of social media.

I will give a brief overview of some of the powerful features of LinkedIn and techniques I suggest you use. My focus will be primarily on the intelligence-gathering part of LinkedIn (although I do suggest you study and use all of the other parts, including how to optimize your profile, the best way to get introduced to others, etc.). Depending on your level of LinkedIn sophistication, this might be painfully elementary—or way over your head. If you are an expert, skim through anyway, you never know what you might pick up. If you're a LinkedIn newbie, do invest the time to raise your level of expertise. It WILL pay off for you.

Here are just a few Smart Calling LinkedIn Tips:

Join LinkedIn Groups. Here you'll find prospects in niche areas, which provide you with somewhat-qualified sources of prospects. To describe simply, a Group is like a big chat room or trade show. As of this writing there were over 1.4 million groups, some with just a few members, with the largest having over 700,000. You'll find groups by industry, job function, and special interests. There very likely are several alumni groups from your high school and college. LinkedIn allows you to join up to 50 groups, and you should take advantage of this capability. Join and monitor groups in your industry and those where your prospects are.

For your Smart Calling, groups are useful in a number of ways. You can monitor member questions and discussions to learn of problems, needs, frustrations, and requests for recommendations for vendors. Sign up to receive a weekly or even a daily digest of what's going on in your groups. You will glean valuable information, which you can then use in your opening statement and/or voice mail message, or in your invitation to connect.

In addition to just seeing, you can be seen as well. Many savvy sales pros participate in discussions and position themselves as experts in their field.

Being a group member also allows you to see more complete prospect information beyond your first-level contacts.

Search LinkedIn Answers. When people have professional questions, whether they be about a business problem or a need for a vendor, many post the question on LinkedIn, either in a forum or the general Answers section. Do a search on the keywords describing the pain you ease, problem you solve, or value you deliver, and you'll likely find someone looking for that answer.

Search LinkedIn Companies. You can get useful information by going to a company's listing, which is a combination of information they input, and what LinkedIn obtains from other sources. You can learn of changes and trigger events, Smart reasons to contact them.

Be an Advanced People-Searcher. Here's a way to have LinkedIn help build your prospect list. To the right of the Search box at the top of your home page, when the People dropdown is selected, click on the Advanced link to the right. You now have a variety of criteria you can use to find prospects matching the profile you desire. For example, I entered "VP of Sales" in the Title box, entered my Postal Code for location, and selected Computer Software for the Industry, and came up with 284 executives that matched my query, a pretty good list to prospect for business in my own backyard. You can further refine your search by keywords, company name, and more. And, get this, LinkedIn will even e-mail you updates based on your search when new contacts match the criteria. It's like LinkedIn is your own sales assistant, In addition to your Google News Alerts assistant, locating prospects for you.

Who's Looking at You? You can see who looked at your profile, which can be a reason to call (preferably coupled with other Smart Calling intelligence). You can also sometimes get a "look back" by viewing a profile, then having them view you out of curiosity.

InMail instead of E-mail. On paid accounts, you can send an internal e-mail through LinkedIn to people who are not first-degree connections. LinkedIn says these are 30 times more likely than a "cold" call to get a response, however Neal Schaffer calls them the "Hail Marys," likening them to the desperate end-of-game, last resort, low-percentage-chance passes in football. Free account users can pay $10 each for these messages, which could be a great investment if it helps you get through and in.

InsideView

If you follow everything I suggest in this chapter, you'd have about sixteen tabs open on your screen before a call just to learn a little bit about a prospect. And I know that many salespeople reading this may not require that level and amount of information, and perhaps they are not even full-time salespeople. However, for those of you whose career is business development, and you are rainmaking day in and day out, it is well worth your time and money investment to utilize a sales intelligence resource.

I'm referring to a web-based service that does most of the research work for you, saving a tremendous amount of time, and getting information you otherwise would not have. There are a number of sales intelligence resources on the market, and InsideView (www.InsideView.com) is the one that is most commonly recognized as a leader. It combines the capabilities of a number of other tools into one powerhouse of information. InsideView gives you a single screen that contains all that information, and it integrates directly with your CRM.

InsideView lines up basic contact data, such as e-mail addresses, phone numbers, and Twitter handles, next to news alerts about trigger events and all the social media buzz surrounding a company or an individual.

InsideView also does a phenomenal job updating their product to stay ahead of new trends. Their Connections feature is really cool, in that it shows how your entire network connects you to a prospect, so you see how your personal contacts, LinkedIn connections, Facebook friends, alumni network, previous employment network, as well as the networks of all your colleagues, connect you to a prospect. This feature allows sales reps to employ referral selling a majority of the time. Like many of the intelligence resources, there is a free version and a premium version.

OneSource iSell

Another leading sales intelligence service, and perhaps the largest competitor of InsideView is OneSource iSell, www.onesource.com/isell. It also provides company and contact information, and identifies trigger events. It combines content from 50 leading suppliers, in addition to thousands of feeds ranging from company data to social media. Triggers are detected from 30 different types of events, ranging from news, financial data changes, and SEC filings.

OneSource iSell was recognized as the best in its category by Top Sales World, winning the Top Sales Productivity Solution of 2010 and 2011. (Top Sales World is the organization that awarded this book Top Sales Book of 2010.)

Blogs

Anyone can blog—and many millions do, even if they have nothing to say (which is often the case). However, if your prospects blog, you can glean some very valuable information to help you connect and hopefully help them buy.

Also, your prospect or your prospect's company might be mentioned in a blog. Again, potentially valuable information that could help you make a connection with your opening or voice mail.

It's worth checking for blogs written by and about your prospect and the company at www.blogsearch.Google.com. (Shameless self-promotion: I also recommend my blog, www.SmartCalling.com, for useful information on Smart Calling and all other aspects of sales.)

Other Free and Paid Online Sources of Information

Here are some of the other more popular sources—both free and fee-based—of information available online. This list is certainly not all-inclusive, so I suggest you check our resource center at www .SmartCalling.com for updates and other informational resources.

Data.com, formerly Jigsaw (which was acquired by Salesforce.com in 2010) is a user-generated database of more than 32 million people (doubled in just three years from the first edition of this book) and their contact information. Each contact lists a phone number and an e-mail address. Many of the contacts have *direct dial* phone numbers—an invaluable resource for Smart Callers.

NetProspex (www.netprospex.com) is similar to Data.com in that it provides contact information that is crowd-sourced. Their differential advantage is that they use humans to call contacts to verify and update information, constantly cleaning their data.

Manta (www.Manta.com) is a free search service that provides company information such as locations, numbers of employees, and estimated revenue figures. (I say "estimated" because that's the case for the search I ran on my company—since I never answer revenue questions when people call seeking that information.)

American City Business Journals (www.BizJournals.com) publishes the local business newspaper in most of the major markets. You can check out this site for national business news, as well as the local news in your city or market. I personally subscribe to the *Phoenix Business Journal,* and it is an invaluable source of local business news and sales leads. In almost every weekly issue, I can find an article that provides a reason to contact a business for a sales opportunity.

It should go without saying that you read the trade publications for your industry *and* those that you sell into. You can find trade journals (http://smallbiztrends.tradepub.com) and subscribe to them for free.

The website www.ZoomInfo.com provides profiles on people and businesses. You can get e-mail addresses and phone numbers here that you might not get elsewhere, without having to "connect" with them first. Like many services there is a free version, and a premium level with enhanced capabilities and value.

A paid service from Dow Jones (www.Factiva.com) provides research and news from a variety of sources on industries, companies, and individuals.

Another paid service (www.Hoovers.com), owned by Dun & Bradstreet, provides relevant, updated information primarily on larger companies.

One of the world's largest research and information providers, LexisNexis (www.LexisNexis.com) offers several paid services specifically for prospecting and relationship development. From the home page, click on Solutions, and then under Business Solutions, click on Sales Professionals to see options that will be especially helpful for you and your industry.

Social Networking—or Social Not-Working?

Another new social networking site probably popped up in the time it took you to read this sentence. Certainly, many of these sites could provide valuable Smart Calling intelligence. Particularly if there are communities devoted entirely to buyers in your industry (similar to the groups on LinkedIn). However, they can also be a tremendous time toilet.

One of the main arguments against using social networking sites for prospecting is that if you are, for example, targeting higher-level buyers, they might not be on these sites. For my money, Dan Kennedy is one of the top marketing and sales minds in the world. In his "No B.S. Marketing Letter," he cited research conducted by the blog www.UberCEO .com that found that *not one Fortune 100 CEO* had a blog, only 2 had Twitter accounts, and a scant 19 had a personal Facebook page. UberCEO claimed that it was "shocking" that so many top CEOs were so disconnected; Kennedy wrote that *he* was shocked that two were actually *using* Twitter—these folks are *busy*. Kennedy says that the higher up the ranks you go in business and affluence, the less use of social media you will find. He explains, "It's really silly to believe any really important, exceptionally productive business leader is devoting time to these things."

Gavin Ingham, (www.GavinIngham.com) a UK-based motivation and sales speaker and author, said it quite well in his own blog:

> What if your clients have not embraced blogs, Twitter, Facebook, etc? In some markets, the lion-share of individuals have not even heard of these sites, they do not read blogs and many over 30 do not even have a Facebook account. To them Twitter is something they do not

understand or see the point of. I know many busy executives who make important buying decisions for companies who are "too busy to mess about on the internet" as they have "a real job to do"!

How do you reach these people through social media?

You don't. Not yet anyway and maybe you never will. Some people do not have the time or interest for social media. Some people do not and might not "get" social media. Social media is incredibly powerful but you cannot use it to reach and engage with people who have not yet embraced it and who do not use it. Social media is powerful but it is not a wonder solution that wipes out all others. Social media is a "communication" channel and as such should only be part of an overall sales and communication strategy.

I can just see some sales managers reading this right now, saying, "That's right! See. We shouldn't be wasting time online on these social media thingies. We need to be pounding the phones, making calls!"

Whoa. Not so fast there, pardner.

There is no denying the explosion in the popularity of social media. Granted, not everyone embraces it. But if you're like me, and are—or were—a resister or late-adopter—keep something in mind:

You are not your customer or prospect.

It doesn't matter how you feel about tweeting or Facebooking, if that's where your customers are, that's where you can get valuable Smart Calling information and should be.

Again, I'm not going to address your overall social media *marketing* strategy. That is a much larger discussion that experts discuss online every day.

What I will discuss is some of the top social media sites you should consider for getting Smart Call sales intelligence. I'll touch on a few resources that I have changed my tune on since the first edition of this book, just three short human years ago, but an eternity ago in the lightning-fast ever-changing digital world.

Twitter

Personally, I took the plunge into Twitter before the first edition of this book (www.Twitter.com/ArtSobczak). I built up my number of followers, and still schedule tweets daily (I know, that really sounds funny). I do keep my posting activity almost exclusively business-related.

For Smart Calling intelligence purposes, you may be able to find useful information about prospects and their ideas, issues, and them personally. In addition, many companies have Twitter accounts, so this could provide useful insight as well that you might be able to use as the basis for a connection.

As part of my routine when researching prospects, I check Twitter to see if they are active. With one prospect, I noticed that she had an account, but only tweeted occasionally. I noticed one where she was on vacation and tweeted that she was thrilled her resort had Skinnygirl Margaritas (a brand name). Of course I wasn't going to lead with that on our initial call, which happened to go very well. Rapport was built, and I was comfortable enough at the end of the call to ask her about Skinnygirl Margaritas. We had a good laugh, which did not hurt the relationship-building. I did get the business.

If you have certain prospects you are coveting, sign up for a service like Hootsuite or Tweetdeck, where you can create private lists of those you'd like to follow and monitor their conversations.

You can also search hashtags to find conversations about specific topics, groups, or interests. (A hashtag is the # followed by the word.) For example, as I was writing this paragraph I did a search on # salestraining. It returned a page of tweets from other sales trainers, but also one from a sales manager who asked, "I'm going to provide webinars for my team. What pitfalls should I avoid?" I will answer that with some good content, and then that provides the basis for a Smart Call.

Also, you can follow prospects you would like to make contact with. Unlike LinkedIn or Facebook where they must accept your invitation to connect, you many follow anyone. You could call them and reference something they had tweeted. Or, you could reply to their tweet and engage in a virtual conversation before contacting them.

Facebook

When I turned in the manuscript for the first edition of this book in November 2009, I wrote: "As for Facebook, I do not use it. My feeling—and that of many others—is that it primarily is more of a true social network, with the majority of use being personal."

Well, that changed even before the book was released in March 2010. By then I had a Facebook fan page and over a thousand followers with many more now. Like Twitter, I don't use it for personal posts, but for sharing business information and collecting Smart Call intelligence, which you should do as well.

Most savvy companies have Facebook pages. When doing your research, check out what you can on their page. You might just uncover a nugget you can use.

Also, when you have names, search for them on Facebook. Since it is more of a personal social network, you might find information that you likely wouldn't see elsewhere. Search their posts, photos, and the things they "Like." Again, just because you find something doesn't mean you will use it. But if you can learn about your prospects' interests in anything and everything such as music, food, sports, hobbies, and gain insight about their beliefs and values, there are a variety of ways that info could be useful for you in making an initial connection, and building a relationship. Plus you might see some cool pictures.

YouTube

I'm not sure if YouTube fits in a social media conversation, but I *am* sure that it is the second-largest search engine, only behind its father, Google. Which means there are a lot of people looking there, and a lot of stuff posted there.

Don't get me wrong; you won't want to waste time viewing videos of dancing cats. (Unless, of course, they belong to your highly-targeted prospect.) But if using video is part of your targeted prospect's business, you could find some real gems.

Video is becoming more popular by the second, and most of us have the capability of shooting and uploading a video at any time with the Smartphone we have in our pocket. I found a brief video of one of my prospects, a sales manager, who gave a brief motivational speech to his team to kick off a sales contest. One of his reps recorded it and uploaded it to YouTube. The guy did a pretty decent job, and I complimented him on a sales call to him. How many salespeople who called on him did the same?

Finally, this should not be a revelation to you: Look at social media as you would any other activity that requires a time investment on your part. Pick the outlets that are most likely to yield good Smart Call intelligence, analyze how much time you need to invest in them, discern what your potential return could be, and create your pre-call planning accordingly.

You now have a clear idea of the information you'd like to have about your prospects before speaking with them, and a number of places you can go to find it. But we're not done yet. Some of the very best information you can get will come from other people. I'll show you how to do this in our next chapter.

Smart Calling Action Steps

What else will you commit to do as a result of this chapter?

Using Social Engineering to Gather Intelligence

The term *social engineering* is most widely used to describe unscrupulous behavior, such as misrepresenting oneself and lying to manipulate someone to provide sensitive information. However, we use it positively and ethically to gather intelligence for our Smart Calls. To us, social engineering simply means talking to people other than your prospect to gather information that will help you help your prospect. It can be done:

As a separate call before your first call to your prospect.

Every time you call your prospect.

I find this to be the most underutilized tool available to salespeople—and the one that has the greatest possible payoff. All it requires is that you take the time to do it, develop a sense of curiosity, and cultivate some conversational questioning techniques. Completing all of these steps may indeed grant you a revelation that many of us have had: People are willing to give you amazing amounts of high-quality information if you *just ask them.*

Kevin Mitnick was one of the most notorious computer hackers in the world, and at the time of his arrest in 1995, the most wanted computer criminal in U.S. history. After his release from prison, he wrote

The Art of Deception (another book I highly recommend), in which he shares precisely how he pulled off many of his hacking jobs. Mitnick claims that he compromised computers solely by using passwords and codes that he gained by *social engineering*, in other words, simply talking to people. Now a speaker and security consultant to corporations, Mitnick points out that the weakest link in any security system is the person holding the information. You just need to *ask* for it.

Of course, we are using social engineering in the positive sense: asking for information from people that will *help* other people and the organization as a whole. The social engineering process for Smart Calling is as follows: Upon reaching a live voice, you:

1. **Identify yourself and the company you represent,** as in, "*Hi, I'm Jason Andrews with National Systems.*" This immediately shows that you are not hiding anything.
2. **Ask for help.** "*I hope you can help me out*" and "*I need some assistance*" are requests that can go a long way. Most people have an innate desire to be helpful to others in some way.
3. **Use a justification statement.** This is the key that will unlock the most useful information. Some examples are:
   a. "*I want to be sure that I'm talking to the right person there.*"
   b. "*I'm going to be speaking with your VP of sales and want to be sure that I have accurate information.*"
   c. "*So that I'm better prepared when I talk to your CIO, I have a few questions you probably could answer.*"
4. **Ask questions.** Of course, you want to ask about the basic, factual material that you might not have information about yet. This depends both on what you sell and on the level of person with whom you're speaking. In general, the higher up you go, the better the quality of information.

The theory behind the success of these justification statements I suggest is discussed by Robert Cialdini—widely considered one of the foremost experts on persuasion and influence—in his classic book, which I believe should be in every serious salesperson's library, *Influence: The Psychology of Persuasion.* Cialdini cites an experiment conducted by Harvard social psychologist Ellen Langer in which students let others cut in line in front of them at the copy machine simply because they provided a reason for their request—"because I'm in a rush."

Direct mail copywriters also employ this technique, often referring to it as the "Why" or the "Because." For example, if a business is running a promotion, they know their response will increase if they give the reason for it. For example, "We need to make room for next year's new models and are clearing out the warehouse, so we are dropping prices to move the current models."

I recommend that you take the time to create your own justification statement—your *because* reason—and use it regularly.

Smart Calling Exercise

1. Prepare your own script for social engineering by using the preceding process. Be sure you have a justification statement you are comfortable with.

2. Brainstorm for the questions you will ask at all levels of an organization, and write them out. (You may want to do this after going through the chapter on questioning.)

With Whom Should You Engage?

Really, you could speak with anyone in a prospective organization. Following are some specific suggestions:

Users of Your Type of Product or Service. An office furniture sales rep told me that he garners valuable information from almost anyone he can get on the phone, since all of the employees use the furniture in the office. He finds out what pieces they have, how old they are, what they have to do when they need something new or replaced, and how functional and comfortable the furniture is. This helps him craft his Possible Value Statement to the decision maker, as well as develop some questions.

Screeners, Gatekeepers, and Assistants. We have an entire chapter on working with these people, not only to get information but also using their help to reach the end buyer. While often looked at as the enemy, we'll discuss why they may wield as much information and power as the buyer.

Sales Department. We know salespeople love to talk, right? If you have a solution that might be able to help a company—and its sales reps—sell more, it's pretty likely that they would be interested and help you with information.

Human Resources. You may be able to collect names of decision makers here by asking questions.

PR or Investor Relations. This is the part of the company *whose job it is* to provide information. If you are coming up empty in trying to locate a name or other information, go to these departments. If you can find a press release, it always has a contact name that can be a starting point in your quest.

Customer Service. This is a group specifically trained to be helpful and answer questions; it's right there in their position title! Don't be afraid to approach these people with your questions; not only do they have a wealth of information on the company but also they are in constant contact with the very group that your prospective client needs to please most: their customers.

Purchasing. You usually don't want to be selling here, since their job is primarily to buy on price. However, you may be able to collect some great information from this group—such as the organization's buying process, from whom they are currently buying, and maybe even what they pay for your type of product or service.

Accounts Payable and Receivable. Again, if you encounter a company that has the policy of not connecting you unless you have a name, in many cases you still can be put through to these departments. However, I am *not* suggesting that you ever misrepresent yourself or your intentions.

Assume What You Can't Get and You'll Always Be Right

Don't automatically assume that a specific type or piece of information is ever *impossible* to get. I sometimes hear salespeople claim, "A secretary wouldn't know anything about the specifics of their technology initiatives," and as a result, the salesperson does not bother to ask a secretary about this topic. The fact is that you'll never know unless you ask. Even if it turns out that the person from whom you are seeking information doesn't have what you're looking for, you didn't lose anything by asking. Plus, people you least suspect to be knowledgeable in a given area may surprise you.

As I mentioned earlier, you want to conduct social engineering on *every* call. Even if you do not reach your decision maker—which, again, will occur most of the time—you will at least have an opportunity to salvage some information from the call.

More Social Engineering Tips

Here are some additional ideas to help with your own social engineering.

Ask Them to Be Your Eyes

When a sales rep is on site at a prospect's or customer's location, it's easy to look around and get clues for sales opportunities. For example, an office equipment or furniture rep could obviously scan an area to get a feel for what the company owns. How can we do that by phone? By asking, of course. In addition to asking a receptionist, admin person, or anyone, for that matter, questions about what they do or use in a product or service category, a label sales rep, for example, could also add something like "Would you please look around and tell me if you see any other imprinted labels anywhere?"

Get on the Approved List First

A sales manager shared an idea that works well with his telesales reps. Companies often have approved vendor lists upon which any seller must be before the prospect could purchase. Instead of following the route that many salespeople take—trying to sell the prospect first—this manager's reps ask the operator or screener if there is an approved vendor list, and if so, how to get on it. The callers follow the appropriate steps. Then, when speaking with the prospect, it's a real door-opener to mention that they're already on the list.

Talk to Other Sales Reps

Many of you reading this are inside sales reps, conducting most of your selling entirely by phone. If there are outside sales reps for your company who sell into your territory or to the same accounts, they can be a great resource for you. Naturally, they know the main buying motivators of typical prospects and customers, and they also can give specific tips about how to handle certain customers and prospects in the field.

An Example of Social Engineering in Action

Let's listen in on a Smart Caller who has gathered some intelligence about her prospect company, has an idea that she ultimately needs to speak with Carl Prentice, the VP of Marketing, and learned from the company operator that Diane Jimenez has the title of Media Buyer.

> KELLY. Diane Jimenez's office, this is Kelly. May I help you?
>
> SMART CALLER. Hi, Kelly, I'm Pam Drayton with Elegant Images. And yes, I'm hoping you can help me.
>
> KELLY. Well, what do you need?
>
> SMART CALLER. I'm going to ask to speak with your VP of Marketing, Carl Prentice, and I wanted to be sure that what we do would be of some value to him.
>
> KELLY. This is Ms. Jimenez's office, she works for him. I can transfer you to his assistant.
>
> SMART CALLER. That will be great, but actually there's information that you could probably help me with. You work closely with her, right?
>
> KELLY. Yes, I'm the admin for her and a few others. Make it quick.
>
> SMART CALLER. I understand Diane handles some of the media buying there.
>
> KELLY. Yes.
>
> SMART CALLER. Can you tell me a few of the markets where you will be focusing your buying for the next quarter?
>
> KELLY. Who are you with again?
>
> SMART CALLER. Elegant Images. We actually help advertisers get more coverage and run more spots at better rates than they usually can get themselves.
>
> KELLY. Oh. We're planning on going into a brand new market for us, the Southwest, Nevada, and Arizona.
>
> SMART CALLER. Wow, that's great. So you've never been there before?
>
> KELLY. No, totally new. I really need to go, want me to transfer you?
>
> SMART CALLER. That's okay. I'll call back, and I actually would like to talk to Diane first. Is she in?
>
> KELLY. No, she'll be back tomorrow.
>
> SMART CALLER. Thanks, Kelly, you've been very helpful. I'll try back tomorrow.

In this brief exchange, the Smart Caller, Pam, accomplished several things:

Confirmed that Diane handled some media buying.

Learned that Diane worked for Carl Prentice, who she feels is the ultimate decision maker for what she is selling.

Very important, scored big by learning that the company is moving into new markets where they have not had experience, precisely the type of situation that would make them a good prospect for Pam.

Built some rapport with Diane's admin, Kelly, and even provided a hint of some value.

Learned that Diane would be back tomorrow and let Kelly know that she will call back. Of course, Pam will not be a stranger then.

Pam will then call back to speak with Diane and treat it as a quasi-social engineering prospecting call, with the goal of finding more information, learning about Diane's needs, getting Diane's buy-in on Pam's services, and perhaps getting Diane's assistance in getting to and selling Carl.

I know as a fact that most sales reps do not go to this level with their questioning. And they are missing opportunities. Granted, not everyone will cooperate with you, and not everyone will have all of the information you seek. So what? On the other hand, just imagine what you could get!

Social Engineering Feedback, and an Answer to an Objection

The success stories I received from sales reps who formerly didn't even think to do anything like Social Engineering has been overwhelming. That's no surprise, because I know it works.

What I also expected, and received were a few objections from doubters, those who resisted using it, suggesting that decision makers would be upset that their employees would share company information, and that as salespeople we could put others in a bad position with their boss for doing so.

Here are my answers to that:

1. Like most things we worry about, it rarely happens.
2. If it does (I have not heard any of those reports) just have this reply ready to roll:

"Oh, well I just wanted to be sure that what I had would be of value to you before I called so I would not be wasting your time like a lot of the calls you might get from salespeople who know nothing about you." Then continue with your call.

Smart Calling Action Steps

What will you commit to *do* as a result of reading this chapter?

Setting Smart Call Objectives and Never Being Rejected Again

U nless you like to joyride in the countryside, you usually don't get in your vehicle and say, "I'm going to start my car, and then just start driving. We'll see what happens." No, you get in your car because you have a very specific destination in mind. Then you figure out what route you need to take to get there. You follow that route, and usually, you arrive.

However, sales reps often take this type of impromptu, poorly prepared approach with their potential clients, and begin prospecting calls like an unfocused driver. They start talking about a given topic but meander around in circles, never ending at a desired destination since they didn't establish one to begin with. Maybe you've had that feeling after a call—the one where you shake your head, thinking, "What just *happened* on that call? I was all over the place."

Begin with the end in mind.

—Habit Two, from Steven Covey,
The Seven Habits of Highly Effective People.

When sitting with sales reps on individual coaching sessions, I always ask for their objectives before calls. I hear such things as:

"I want to see who they're buying from now."
"I'd like to qualify and send out some info."
"I want to see if they have any needs."

None of those are primary objectives. Granted, they should all be accomplished, but none are the end *result* you're ideally looking for on a call. *That* is your primary objective.

In order to maximize your chances for success on your calls, you need to begin by setting and focusing on the end result you desire. I define your primary objective as what you want the person on the other end to *do* as a result of the call—emphasis on the *do*. It must be action-oriented.

The ultimate primary objective, of course, is to get them to buy at the end of this call. But this can vary in terms of the specific action taken. Perhaps your objective is to "get agreement that the customer will take your proposal to the board meeting and recommend its approval." Maybe you want to qualify, generate interest, and get the prospect to agree to do a side-by-side comparison between his existing product and yours. Or maybe you want to secure a promise that they will take part in a web demo.

Look at these again. They all involve your prospect *doing* something.

Let's test your understanding of a primary objective. Look at each of these and determine if they are a suitable primary objective.

Smart Calling Exercise

1. I want to find out what system they're using now to track client time and billing for their legal work.
2. I want to identify a compelling need that I can fill.
3. I want to get set an appointment with the prospect, assuming he is qualified, and get him to include other influencers in the meeting.

Answers

1. Not a primary objective. The rep *would* want to find that out, but then what? That would be the *do* we want them to perform.
2. Not. Again, while we do want to accomplish that, we also want the prospect to take some action as the result of the call.
3. Yes! The prospect is agreeing to meet with the sales rep and bring other influencers to the meeting.

Thinking Big Gets Big Results

As long as you are thinking anyway, think big.

—Donald Trump

When establishing your primary objective, think *big*. One thing's for sure: If you aim low, you'll rarely hit above your target. When you aim high, you'll sometimes reach it and, on average, will achieve greater results than if you start low.

I suggest that you adopt the attitude that all elite athletes have regarding your call objectives. Michael Phelps *expected* to win every time he dove into the pool. Why wouldn't *you* do the same and expect to achieve the ultimate on every call you make?

So what expectations do you set as you prepare your prospecting calls? Some sales reps who approach calls "just to see if there might be any interest there" are often surprised when they stumble upon someone who actually stays on the phone with them. But they become uneasy with their brief success, not wanting to take the call too far, and quickly jump off the call, saying, "Well, let me send you out some information, and I'll call back again"—wasting an opportunity in the process.

High achievers, on the other hand, expect to take the call as far as possible, and they do. They begin calls with a specific, ambitious objective, whether it is the sale or the appointment.

I often ask in my sales training seminars about the furthest anyone has ever gone on a prospecting call. Even in higher-ticket, more complex sales situations, there are extraordinary success stories about the guy who made a sale on a prospecting call. And for some of you, that is routine. So therefore, in those situations, it is *possible*. And if it's possible, why not make that your objective on every call? Even if you don't reach it—which might be most of the time—you'll still consistently reach higher levels than you would have otherwise. And think about how much time you can save by moving prospects to a decision more quickly, regardless of what that decision ultimately is.

Approach every call anticipating the fulfillment of the highest conceivable end result. You won't get there *every* call, but you know what? Your results over time will be much higher than they would be with low—or no—expectations.

So here's your mission: For every call you place from here on out, simply ask: "What do I want this person to *do* as a result of this call?" That's your primary objective.

Smart Calling Exercise

Write out your primary objective for the prospect you are working on.

How to Never Be Rejected Again: Accomplishing Your Secondary Objective

No one can make you feel inferior without your consent.
—Eleanor Roosevelt

Some of you undoubtedly purchased this book simply because of the subtitle and the part about "eliminating rejection" from your calls. Follow my advice, and you will not be disappointed or feel rejected ever again.

First, we need to put some things in perspective. If you have ever felt—or feared—rejection on a prospecting call, what is it exactly that you heard, or feared hearing?

Oh, I know the answers:

"We are happy with what we are using."
"We don't need that."
"We're all set."
"Not interested."
"No thanks."
"No."

And there are more, of course.

What's interesting, though, about most of what incites these feelings of rejection is that these are things that happen *to* you. This begs another question: Is rejection what happens to you, or is it the *way you react to it*?

Rejection, as it turns out, is always your *reaction* to the response that you receive.

Smart Calling Key Point

Remember: No one can reject you without your consent.

Let's look at two sales reps, both of whom just heard a no on a call. The first rep thinks, *Geez, another no. This rejection is getting to me. Rejection sucks. What's wrong with me? It's depressing. I think I'll go check what's in the vending machine.*

The second rep says, *Oh, well. He wasn't a prospect today. I did ask him if we could keep the door open for the future, and he agreed to receive our e-mail newsletter. Another small win—on to the next one!*

While they both got a similar no, one sales rep salvaged something from the call. At the end of the prospecting day, the first rep feels beaten bloody because he tells himself that he has been the victim of constant rejection. The other rep says, *Well, I accomplished my primary objective three times today, and the rest of the time I accomplished my secondary. Pretty good day!*

Unless you proactively look for and achieve wins—regardless of how small—you will be pulled down by prospecting. Therefore, for your Smart Calling mental health, you need to set a secondary objective for every call, which is, *What you can attempt, at minimum, on your calls.*

Notice that this does not have to be a *do* on their part; it can simply be an attempt that you make. In the event that you do not accomplish your primary objectives, possible secondary objectives could be:

"I want to leave them with a good feeling about my company."

"I want to ask who they are now buying their supplies from."

"I will ask if I could recontact them in the future."

This is not high-level stuff; it doesn't need to be. It is for your attitude.

Secondary Objectives Can also Pay Off in the Future

An extra bonus with a secondary objective is that it can be a seed that you harvest later. For example, a travel agency sales rep cold-called me, using the old alternate-choice close to try to set an appointment: *"So I'd like to come out there and tell you what we do. Would Thursday or Friday be better?"*

I quickly replied that I was not a prospect for him. He then surprised me by responding brilliantly: *"Oh?"* It was brilliant, because it got me talking. I proceeded to tell him I was happy with my present agency, that I had actually used his agency before, and that the new agency was able to do things that his agency couldn't at the time because of their size. I even told him more, all as a result of that one word. He responded that he understood but asked that if anything ever happened with my present agency, could he be the first in line to be considered—especially given that I had worked with them before (prior to his arrival there).

Fair enough, I told him. As he was taking down my information to send me his card, he slipped in another question: *"Kind of curious—what would have to happen that would be so severe that would cause you to even consider someone else?"*

Now *that* was even more brilliant, and it got me thinking. I hadn't really established those criteria before. After some pondering, I said that I would probably reconsider my patronage if they gave me a feeling of indifference, since I was a small deal compared to their big accounts. But the major reason would be if they did something that cost me money and would not fix it.

The rep ended by saying, *"I understand. Let me just leave you with two thoughts. You would be a big account for us. We specialize in your size of account. In fact, not only would you have your own personal agent but also all of our agents are cross-trained on two other profiles, so you would always have someone here who knows you. And for the second point, well, it's our president's personal philosophy that doing business with us will never cost our clients money. So we will always make it right."*

Impressive, I thought. He sent me his card and I filed it, but I didn't think much about him for about a year.

Then, several months later, I was running late getting to the airport for a flight from Phoenix to Omaha that I had to be on—it was the last one out that day. (This was pre 9/11, when you could pretty much show up at the gate anytime and still get on the plane without having to wait in lines and endure full body cavity searches, like today.) As I was running through the gate area—still two away from mine—I yelled to the still-distant gate agent before she closed the door to the Jetway, *"Wait, I'm on that flight!"*

Out of breath, I handed her my ticket and thanked her for holding the door. My heart dropped when she looked at me and said, *"I'm sorry, this ticket was for yesterday. I'll need to close the door."*

I told her that was impossible because I had bought a bunch of tickets the prior week, and I even pulled out my yellow legal pad showing all of the flight dates, times, and numbers I had given the agency. She was unimpressed with my notes, but I managed to convince her to let me on the flight—at an additional cost of $600 for the last seat they had on the plane. It was in first class—which I didn't enjoy as much as I usually do.

The next day I called my agent, ranting about how they made a mistake, it cost me $600, and what were they going to do for me? She calmed me down, checked my record, and commented that I had called the prior week and didn't speak with her, my regular agent, because she was gone. I worked with a trainee.

"Well, there's your problem," I announced.

"Actually, it's not our problem. You know it's your responsibility to check your tickets."

She was right. But you know what? The next time I needed to buy a ticket—who do you think I called? I found the card of the guy who had called me a year earlier. I remember what he said about their agency always having someone who would know me, and how doing business with them would never cost me money. And they gained a new client in the process from something he said at the end of a call, during which he did not set an appointment—that had taken place a full year earlier!

You can have the same effect on potential clients that he did on me: You can plant seeds, many of which you might harvest later. And that also can be part of your secondary objective. Remind them of any future, unfavorable circumstances they should look out for—which just might happen to include any problems you could solve. For example:

"Matt, even though there is not a fit today, if you find that your volume gets to the point where it would make sense to outsource your peak-level jobs, keep in mind that we can turn those around quickly for you."

"If more of your customers ask for the type of unit we produce and you have to refer them elsewhere, please remember that we can help you help those customers and realize those profits that you would be missing."

"Okay, Shelley, it doesn't look like I have a fit for what you need today. Here's something to keep in mind, though. When you do notice more of your direct mailings being returned because of bad addresses, we do have a software program that could help you reduce that number and save the

printing and postage expense. I'll send you my card, and please keep it in the file you work from when you're planning mailings, okay?"

Notice the last sentence in the final example. It asks, or tells, prospective clients to place the card (or literature) in a place they'll see it when they're most likely to need it. Do the same with your calls. Tell whomever you're speaking with to put it in their Rolodex under Widgets, in their project file, in their contact management program—anywhere that they can easily access it when they need it. We've all had people we've long written off call us and say, *"Things have changed. Let's talk."* This is a way to make that happen more often.

So, your secondary objective has two major benefits:

1. It ensures that you will never be rejected again, because you will always have some type of a win.
2. It allows you to plant seeds that you might harvest later.

Smart Calling Exercise

Write out your secondary objective for your prospect.

Smart Calling Action Steps

What else will you commit to *do* as a result of this chapter?

6

More Smart Ideas for Prior to Your Call

L et's look at a few other important points to follow prior to picking up the phone, and answer some common questions as well.

Is There a Best Time to Call?

Over the past 30-plus years, I've seen my share of sales studies that claim to show the average number of calls it takes to set an appointment, to close a sale, how long calls should be, and more. And most of them don't mean squat to you or me.

Are you kidding me? Common sense tells you that the guy setting appointments for highly specialized enterprise-level engineering software that is purchased once every 5 to 10 years isn't going to have the same results as the person prospecting to sell subscriptions to the local business journal. I want to scream in frustration when I see these types of "average number of calls to make a sale" and other general stats because there really is no average.

I'm regularly contacted by reps and managers who are seeking my estimate on a metric for some aspect of sales, usually so that they can justify something to their boss. I always tell them there is no way I could offer a number or opinion unless I knew almost everything about their business and situation. The process of sales is not an exact science; there are too many variables involved. What you do relates very little to the guy selling a totally different product or service, to a different market, in a different way. And even if your situations might be somewhat similar, you need to factor in the hugest variable of all: the person doing the selling.

While researching a number of topics for this book, I ran across an article (on www.SellingPower.com) citing a study by Dr. James Oldroyd at the Kellogg School of Management. By looking at the records of more than a million cold calls—made by thousands of salespeople from about 50 companies—he applied some statistical measurements to determine success and failure patterns.

Okay, that got my attention. Oldroyd found that:

- Thursday is the best day to contact a lead.
- Thursday was 20 percent better than the worst day, Friday. Other days were in the middle somewhere.
- Between 8 AM and 9 AM is the best time to call, with between 4 PM and 5 PM the next best choice. (The 8 AM to 9 AM time frame was 164 percent better than a 1 PM to 2 PM call.)

Interesting. What the article did not mention: What were these salespeople saying on their calls? If we took a group of reps trained in Smart Calling who are saying and doing the right things consistently—would they have more success on Friday than the other test group on Thursday? Would they have the same results by calling at different times of the day?

What bothers me is that there probably are sales reps who would read this study—like so many before it—and consequently call only during the stated best times, assuming that the other times are worthless or less productive—and using it as a reason to not call.

Here is my finding, based on over 30 years of unscientific experience attending the School of Real World Observation and Calling:

- If you are not calling, you are not uncovering opportunities. Brilliant, huh?

Now, of course, there are certain industry-specific times that might be better—and worse—for calling. Common sense would tell you not to call a restaurant at lunch time. And the only chance you might have of reaching a building contractor while he's actually in the office is at 6 AM or sometime after dark. Even Dr. Oldroyd agrees: "It's absolutely vital to measure and analyze your own sales data to see what's working and what's not."

Smart Calling Success Story

If you call people who work in industrial environments, Mike Turner at Womack Machine has an idea about how to effectively reach them. Since they're typically out on the plant floor, they're normally not around phones, and paging them could stir up a hornet's nest. However, many of them are around their offices at the beginning of the day, around break times and lunch, and right before quitting time. You can often learn exactly when these times are from receptionists, or you can use this formula: A break is usually two hours after starting time, with lunch two hours after that. So, what is the best time for you? I don't know. What I do know is that you should set aside uninterrupted time, regularly, to do your Smart Calling.

Ritualize Your Phone Time

You might have an interest in Smart Calling for a variety of reasons. Some people might be desperate to generate short-term cash and need to make things happen quickly just to keep the doors open. Maybe you are not in traditional sales, but you are job-hunting and looking for opportunities and interviews. New sales reps perhaps need to shake the bushes to open fresh accounts and build their book of business, with the goal of not needing to rely on prospecting as much in the future. Or the savvy sales pro realizes that prospecting is the key to continually beating his numbers and income goals each year.

Wherever you are, the best method I have seen for someone in prospecting mode is ritualizing your calling. That means making an appointment with yourself to call during set times to which you commit on a regular basis. For some, it must be every day between certain hours, no exceptions. For others, it can be one day a week. Though it will inevitably vary from one person to the next, the key is setting the time—and then doing it.

When I decided more than five years ago that I was going to get back into the shape, weight, and jeans size that I was during my days as a high school athlete, I knew I had to make changes and a commitment to rituals. I had always been in pretty good shape my adult life (with a couple of 20-pound exceptions that came and went); I worked out at home with all of the equipment, including the $14,000 machine you see in airline magazines. But to really get back into 18-year-old condition, I decided that I needed to get into a gym routine with both weights and cardio. And I did. I ritualized it. At least five days a week, sometimes six, I still make it to the gym—usually between 5:30 and 6 AM. I also manage to find the time to work out on the many days when I am on the road doing training. Sure, there are mornings when the bed feels a bit too good, or perhaps I'm a bit hung over and I feel like saying, "Screw it." But we all know how easy it is to let that turn into *Screw it!* again the next day, and the next. . . .

The same rules should apply when you are calling: do it regularly, and do nothing else during that time. Don't check e-mail. Don't write proposals. If you can, do most of your pre-call planning in advance, although I know that may not always be possible. You'll benefit by being completely in the zone, where your energy and momentum builds. Success breeds success. Action builds momentum, and it is motivating. Don't break it with administrative tasks. Your commitment to success will dictate your own rituals, which in turn will produce your results.

When You Are on a Roll, Stay in the Zone

Want to know the absolute best time to place calls? When you are in your own personal success zone. That's the magic time when you have a string of very successful calls, your attitude is at a peak, and—almost magically—everything falls in your favor.

One of the greatest baseball hitters ever, Ted Williams, said that when he was on a hitting streak (which was often) he could see the rotation of the seams on a baseball traveling more than 90 miles per hour. Hall of Famer George Brett said the ball looked as big as a beach ball coming in. You also probably have some way to describe that great feeling you have when you're on a roll, and successes are coming for you at every turn. So when you're on a personal hot streak—keep going! Don't stop to dwell on the success too long. Take advantage of the groove that you're in and keep plugging away. Try to beat your best results ever. Success has an uncanny way of piling up when you are in a zone.

End with a Positive

Before hitting the machines at the gym, I always shoot some baskets to warm up. I've continued a particular practice I had long ago in high school when I played basketball and later, when I coached my kids' teams: Always be sure your last shot of the day goes in. It might sound like a little thing, but I find it lets me end on a positive note. Similarly, when I was an inside sales rep more than 30 years ago for AT&T Long Lines in corporate life, cranking out numerous calls daily, I had the same rule: End every day with a call that was a win. It was not necessarily a sale, but it was an accomplishment of an objective. Try it! It helps you end your day on a high note and begin the next day the same way.

Smart Calling Exercise

What time rituals are you willing to commit to right now?

Great Days to Call: When Others Aren't or Won't

Want to avoid the call clutter? Call when others won't, or during what they claim to be a bad time: around holidays, summer vacations, and long weekends. Many people traditionally write off these times—either by taking official vacation days or by mentally taking off, even though they are physically present (by showing up at the office and goofing off). However, business is still taking place. Granted, some prospects may not be in. But how is that any different from calling when they *are* in and reaching voice mail?

But other buyers are working. And maybe their gatekeepers are out. Perhaps it's more relaxed in their office, and they are more apt to pick up the phone during these times. Maybe they're even in a better mood, since everyone isn't banging their doors down, wanting something.

Be sure to call during the week between Christmas and January 1. There are buyers with money to spend before the end of the year. Maybe there's money left in the budget, or perhaps they need to spend for tax purposes. If they're presented with an intriguing offer during this time, they just might be more apt to make a buying decision. I personally buy more for business in late December than during any other month because

I need to reduce my tax burden. So I load up on things I'll need over the next year.

I've never really understood people's tendency to avoid calling during this particular week. What do these people think? That when they get back to the office on January 2 and start hitting the phones, they'll be the only ones with that idea? No! *Everyone* starts calling the first day back in the office. And that's the very day that decision makers are swamped with their own work!

You might not be hitting it hard during these traditional downtimes because you're assuming that you probably won't reach many people. But here's all that you know for sure during that time:

If you're *not* placing calls, you have *no* chance of reaching these people and selling to them.

Over the years, I have collected many success stories of reps catching up with that otherwise hard-to-reach decision maker and starting a business relationship during this so-called dead week. Here's one.

Smart Calling Success Story

The last two weeks of December were our best weeks ever last year. The team made a decision in their minds that they would use the holidays and end of year as a reason to close up deals instead of a reason to get put off for later. It worked! My team performed 14 percent better than the average for the previous six months.
—Travis Isaacson, Sales Manager, Access Development

Other Unconventional Times to Call

After or before Hours

Who's normally working late or coming in early? Owners, executives, people who control money. A rep selling computer printer supplies once told me about how he had called into the corporate franchise headquarters of Subway sandwich shops late in the evening, thinking he would get voice mails so that he could ferret through the system and glean some information. Instead, he found a guy who answered a ringing extension and entered into a conversation. The man was a VP in the IT department and put the rep in touch with the person who subsequently became a customer.

Weekends

I know most people won't take the time and give up their weekend—or even a portion of it—to make phone calls. But some will—and they will reach buyers, C-levels, and owners who are in their office and whose screeners are not working. They are more relaxed during these times and can take more time to listen to you and, therefore, buy from you.

Bad Weather Days

Pay attention to the weather in areas that you call into. I know of reps who make it a point to call in areas that have just been hit with a blizzard during the winter.

In his sales book *Can I Have 5 Minutes of Your Time?* Hal Becker details the experience of a Xerox sales rep who set a record during a three-day snowstorm, while many of the businesses in his city were closed. Most of the gatekeepers stayed home during this time, but their bosses were in. Many of these were prospects he had tried to reach, unsuccessfully, in the past. This particular rep set a 3-day record for sales that lasted more than 25 years!

Best Times for Follow-up Calls

I'm going to jump ahead a bit here to a later stage in the prospecting cycle. After you have gathered some information from an assistant about the best time to reach the buyer—or have actually spoken with him yourself—set a specified field set aside in your computer (or another consistent spot in your notes) that indicates the best times to call for this particular client. If you call the same people on a routine basis, knowing when you have a better chance of reaching them can save you a lot of time—time that you can then allocate to making more Smart Calls and sales. People are creatures of habit, and you are far more likely to catch a given person at the same time each day. If you haven't reached certain clients successfully yet, try calling a different time of day on each attempt you make. This will increase your chances of hitting them at the right time this way.

Warming Up a Smart Call

If you, a staff member, or a marketing person can warm up your calls by sending something in advance—something that can possibly acquaint them with you and perhaps create some interest—then by all means, do so! However, don't get your hopes up that anyone will necessarily open or remember what you sent. (Ask high-level decision makers in your company how much unsolicited mail they get and what happens to it.) So why do it? *If* it is targeted and relevant, it can have a significant return on investment.

My friend and fellow sales trainer Bill Lee (www.BillLeeOnline.com) suggests a good idea: Put your prospect on your mailing list long before you make your first call. Of course, this requires some work and planning on your part, but again, if you are serious about this and make Smart Calling a systematic habit, then it will become a ritual for you. Bill suggests sending things that you feel the prospect might find useful (*useful* is the key term here; don't send purely self-promotional propaganda), such as:

- News clippings
- Magazine articles
- Copies of web pages with interesting info
- Helpful hints pertaining to their business
- Your company's newsletter (again, the more about them, the better)

And let me add to the list:

Books: Find general, current, popular business books. Include a brief note about how you thought the prospect might find this interesting and that you will be contacting him soon to discuss some ideas. Sound too expensive? Of course, you wouldn't send these out by the thousands, but let's say a book is $15. I bet you'd have a better chance of getting in to see a high-level prospect when you say to the executive assistant, "I'm the guy that sent the book." When this prospect becomes a client, you'll make that $15 many times over.

Audio CDs or video DVDs: Similar to a book; be sure it is something educational, topical, and of value that will pique interest and curiosity.

Greeting cards: A very persistent sales pro sent me personalized greeting cards every month for 16 months (that's right—16!) while I continually evaded his phone calls. I finally agreed to take some time to listen to the automated system he was using for sending out the personalized cards.

The best time to send the items is after you have already done some social engineering. This allows you to tailor what you send to the prospect's interests and then enlist her assistant in helping you get it to the buyer. And when you do call, you still want to follow all of the steps in the Smart Calling system. Do *not*—I plead with you—do *not* start out your call with "I sent you a letter, did you get it?" (We will cover the opening statement in Chapter 9.)

E-Mailing before a Call

E-mails before a Smart Call can warm up prospects, if structured well. I recently received an e-mail that did catch my attention. It started out: *"Art, thought you might be interested in hearing about how another sales trainer like you was able to get new customers and maintain them at a high lifetime value. . . ."*

Then he went on to share a success story, mentioned some of my services and how they were similar, and shared some testimonials. He said he would call me.

That message earned my time because it was personalized, not just in name, but in content. He did his homework. He also built credibility by using a testimonial with an example of someone like me. Very nice.

This can work also with a hard-copy letter. Again, the key is personalizing the e-mail and subject line using Smart information and not trying to sell in the document.

Multimedia Messages

There's no question that every day video is becoming more prevalent in all types of messages. I've seen it used a variety of ways in e-mails by salespeople, and it can be effective in getting through to a buyer. The problem though, inhibiting its widespread use by sales pros has been the relative difficulty to quickly, easily, and inexpensively send multimedia messages as part of a salesperson's daily routine. However, I recently started using a cool service that removes the obstacles and enables you to quickly create multimedia messages you send in an e-mail.

With PointAcross (www.BusinessbyPhone.com/point-across), from my computer in just a minute or two I can quickly record a message in my voice and create customized slides, along with an image of my prospect I grab from their LinkedIn profile—talk about personalization! I send that in an e-mail, and can monitor when it is viewed. As you can imagine, this is much more effective than a basic e-mail.

How about Sending Unusual Items Prior to the Call?

Donnie Deutsch—host of a show formerly on CNBC called *The Big Idea*—tells the story of when he was building his ad agency and he wanted the account of a regional car dealer. To get to the person who was in charge of awarding the contract, he shipped an assortment of individual car parts to the guy's house every half-hour for a 12-hour period. Each part was accompanied with a different message, like "We'll Give You Bright Ideas" (a headlight), "We'll Protect Your Rear End" (fender), and "We'll Steer You in the Right Direction" (steering wheel). In total, Deutsch sent 24 of these packages. He got the account.

There is no doubt that sending unconventional items to buyers can get their attention. I put these things into the gimmick category. Just like a trick play in football, they make for a sexy story, and they are fun when they work, but you are unlikely to build a career on them. Here are just some of items I have seen and heard about:

- Packages of coffee and a mug: "I'd like to have a cup of coffee with you to discuss some ideas about. . . ."
- Shoes, or blow-up feet. "I'm trying to get my foot in the door."

Lumpy mail. Direct mail marketers know that a three-dimensional envelope gets opened before standard direct mail. You are limited only by your imagination. Oriental Trading Company (www.OrientalTrading .com) sells all kinds of fun things.

A sales rep with Troy XCD Inc., named Angie Medina said that to really differentiate herself, she sends a crumpled-up catalog or brochure in an envelope and attaches a note saying, "Don't throw this away again!"

At a marketing seminar I once attended, one of the participants shared the method he has used to seize the attention of high-level decision makers. I thought that I had heard most of the gimmick-related techniques of sending odd objects to decision makers, but this one beat them all. This salesperson purchases cheap, $20 disposable cell phones (the kind you can get at Walmart). He then sends them to his highly targeted top-level decision makers, along with a note that says, "*I Believe We Can Help You Increase Your Profits. I Will Call You At 3:00 pm On Thursday The 16Th. Please Listen For My Call.*" Then he calls the cell number! He claims that it is so unusual that it works almost every time.

Again, if you are having a difficult time getting through to a buyer—someone you feel you must have as a customer—and have exhausted all of your other avenues, you have nothing to lose by trying an unconventional approach.

Get Direct Numbers

There's no arguing that having a prospect's direct number will get you through more often than having to navigate through an automated system or an assistant. Plus, it saves you time.

The question then is how to get direct numbers.

In Chapter 3, where we talked about sales intelligence resources, many of the premium services provide direct dial phone numbers—yet another reason to invest in them.

In Chapter 4, as part of your social engineering you can and should ask for direct numbers. As a quick tip, when asking for a direct number, do not be shy about it or come across like you are doing something diabolical. Very confidently say, "And what is her direct number?"

Wildcard Searches

You can use the Internet in creative ways to find direct numbers. In Google searches the "*" is known as a "wildcard" character, meaning that when you do not know the number, enter in the asterisk along with whatever information you do have about your prospect, and you might just get lucky.

For example, let's say using LinkedIn you found a prospect you want to target. Simply copy and paste their LinkedIn name and title into Google, then the area code and wild cards, such as 480-***-****. Bingo, chances are you just got a direct line. And, your chances will even go up if you know the phone number prefix, which you can find from their site.

Sam Richter, author of *Take the Cold Out of Cold Calling*, also told me that once you have the direct line, you can enter that into another search along with the name, and chances are you will get the e-mail. Or, if you know the e-mail, that can help you get the direct number.

Let Their Voice Message System Tell You

My friend, Steve Richard, with the sales prospecting and training firm Vorsight, shared this tip with me, which we also published in my Telephone Prospecting and Selling Report newsletter:

> The next time you hear that when you're on someone's voice mail, "Your call is being answered by Audix," punch in **6. It will say "enter last

name, followed by pound sign." Put in their last name, and it will give you their name and extension. Now that you have that magic 10 digit direct dial number, once we dial that, we have a much high probability of having a live conversation with the senior executive.

Smart Calling Action Steps

What else will you commit to *do* as a result of this chapter?

Creating and Placing the Smart Call

How to Be Smart with Voice Mail

Would you like the secret to perfecting that one voice mail message *guaranteed* to get all of your calls returned?

Yeah, I would, too. Let me know if you find it.

Oh, there *are* messages that can get calls returned all the time. There are the ones saying that you're from the IRS and have some important information. Or that you're with the hospital lab department and located something disturbing in some past test results that were overlooked. (As tongue-in-cheek as I am when joking about these, I have, regrettably, seen those techniques suggested before. Sad. And somewhat desperate.)

First, let's get real regarding voice mail and telephone prospecting: You need to lower your expectations. Do not *expect* your calls to be returned.

Come on, now. It's a bit absurd to think that someone who does not know you—who is probably overworked and underpaid, who has 79 unread e-mail messages and 12 other voice mails from people he *does* know—is going to return *your* call. Unless the prospect has an immediate, urgent need and pain that your product or service can address at that very moment, it's much more likely that he will *not* call you.

A couple of years ago, after an overnight torrential downpour, I went down the stairs into the lower level of my house for an early morning workout. At the last step, my foot squished into wet carpet. Oh no! The sump pump had fried, and the lower level of my house was now flooded, with water still gurgling in. At that moment, I would have immediately returned a voice mail message from someone who did sump pump installation or water damage cleanup (unfortunately, I instead spent time waiting for them to return *my* call).

Therefore, the first question we need to answer is: "Should you even leave a voice mail on a Smart Call?" And the very definite answer is "Yes!"

Why? Because you have already done the heavy lifting by completing the intelligence gathering. You know something about the person you're calling, the company, industry, and hopefully its needs, pains, problems, and initiatives. You have a Possible Value Proposition for them. You now have the opportunity to make an impression with your message. Of course, you want to do it correctly, since most voice mail messages create resistance and quickly get zapped.

My suggestion for your voice mail objective is to pique their curiosity with a hint of possible value and leave a question in their minds like: "Hmmm, what exactly might that be?" Or "I wonder how they do *that?*" You want whomever you are contacting to eventually take your call when it is announced by an assistant or perhaps when they see your company name on caller ID.

But what should that message be? It should be almost identical to the interest-creating opening statement that you will be developing in Chapter 10. After all, why would you say something different on voice mail than when you speak with your contacts in person?

Using the Smart Call opening example from Chapter 10, here is a sample voice mail message:

> "Hi, Michael, I'm Pat Stevens with Insurance Partners. Hope you enjoyed your golf vacation. In speaking with your assistant, Suzanne, I understand that you are in the process of evaluating your competitive edge in the employment market and figuring out how to attract and keep the top talent in your various locations. We've been able to help other companies in the same situation lower their recruiting and hiring expenses, and increase their retention of managerial staff. I'd like to ask a few questions to see if I could provide you some information. I'll try you again on Friday morning. If you'd like to reach me in the meantime, my number is 555-###-####. I'll repeat that, 555-###-####. And my e-mail is Pat@IPartners.com. Thanks."

Some might read this and claim that it is long, but long is a matter of perception. Hearing two sentences about opera is too long for me, personally. Call me an uncultured oaf, but I don't care about opera. But if I heard 15 minutes about a barbecue brisket recipe that might be tastier and tenderer than the one I use in competitions, well, that might not be long enough. The bottom line: If the information is on a topic the person is interested in, then a detailed message won't be considered too long.

Smart Calling Key Point

A voice mail message or opening statement is only too long when everything in it is not of interest to the listener. Edit your voice mails and openings in the preparation stage with this in mind.

To repeat: An effective voice message is almost identical to your interest-creating opening statement. The only difference is that at the end, you inform the person you're calling that *you* will call back, and then leave your contact information—just in case they get the urge to call you. Because it is virtually identical to your opening, all of the same rules apply for what to avoid and what works. While I will not repeat them here, I suggest you do review and follow them. If you want to jump ahead, go to Chapter 10.

Smart Calling Exercise

After you complete your opening statement in Chapter 10, come back and modify it slightly by using the ideas here to make it your voice mail message to that prospect.

Following are a few other pointers and tips specifically for maximizing your voice mail effectiveness.

Be Prepared

Here's one of the biggest "Well, duh, no kidding" tips in the book. You have to be prepared to reach voice mail, since this will probably be the case most of the time. But as basic as this is, you'd be surprised to find that it isn't something that sales reps usually do. More often than not, too many simply wing it.

Voice mail is not new technology; it shouldn't be a surprise that you will be asked to speak after the tone. So why wouldn't you be 100 percent prepared for what you'll say? (Just notice how many messages you get that begin with, "Uhhh.") There's no excuse to not be totally smooth and confident. Again, this will stem from your interest-creating opening, which you will have prepared word-for-word—so it shouldn't be a problem for you.

Say You'll Call Back

I have to laugh when I receive prospecting call messages where reps say, *"So please call me at 555-123-4567. I will be in the office and waiting for your call."* They are all still waiting.

As the prospector, *you* need to control the communication. It's your responsibility to reach *them*. Tell them you'll call back Thursday morning—then *do* it. But do give them options to reach you, leaving your phone number and e-mail address—just in case they do opt to contact you.

How Many Messages to Leave?

How many voice mails *should* you leave? I've seen all kinds of formulas. Three calls. Five calls. Eight calls? I don't know. How important is this prospect to you? You have to be the judge.

I do know, however, that if you only call once, you have little chance of ever speaking with your prospect. Even if someone does return the occasional voice mail from a prospector—which, again, is rare—who do they call? Probably not the one-time caller.

A buyer I interviewed told me that he never returns calls and that the only sales reps who have even a remote chance of getting through his screener next time are those he recognizes as having left several interesting voice mails. Personally, I never return first calls from prospectors. I want to see that they are interested enough in doing business with me to be persistent.

Smart Calling Success Story from the Field

"I've been doing two things that seem to have increased my response when I leave voice mails (although I'm guilty of going on too long). First, I will tell the people that I am sending an e-mail with more information. That also means that they know they have my contact information sitting in their inbox, and some people just communicate better by e-mail."

Four seems to be my magic number for voice mail messages; I always seem to get a response to the fourth message. I usually will leave a voice mail on cold calls, which builds its own name recognition. When I do finally get a hold of the people, my name may sound familiar simply because they've heard it three times on their voice mail."

—Toni Spitzman, *The Bulldog Reporter*

Should You Vary Your Message On Repeat Calls?

Why *would* you? Didn't you put a lot of thought into crafting and perfecting your Possible Value Statement? And you did your Smart Call research and used that in the message, right? So changing it would be dumb. After all, even when Kentucky Fried Chicken changed their name to KFC, their slogan stayed the same: "Finger Lickin' Good." Every time you leave a voice mail, you are making another repetitive imprint in the listener's mind. Radio advertisers do this on commercials by repeating a product name or benefit several times.

Plus, let's not be so naïve as to assume that your prospect is going to remember everything you say in a message. I once conducted a training program where the reps called their manager's voice mail and left the message they used on prospecting calls. Here was a revelation: I always had them play the message a second time, immediately after hearing it once. I heard things the second time I had not picked up on, despite having just listened to it seconds earlier. And I was focused on the message, specifically looking for things in the message—much more so than a prospect would be. So create your value-packed message, and use it repeatedly.

Listen to Their Entire Voice Mail Message

I was recently sitting in with a sales rep listening to calls when I noticed a pattern: As soon as the voice mail answered, he always hung up. After he did this about 10 times, I asked him why. *"Leaving messages is a waste of time. So I just hang up as soon I get voice mail."* He also said he tried back three more times over the next week, and if he never reached the person, he simply discarded the name.

I instructed him to call back the previous voice mail he just hung up on, and he did. The prospect's greeting said:

> *"Hi, this is Kevin Davis. For the month of May, I will be working in my Boston office. If you would like to reach me there directly, call 617-###-####."*

The rep rolled his eyes a bit as I gave him an "I told you so" look. He apparently knew nothing about the other location. He then dialed the number, immediately reached the prospect, and entered into a sales process with him. And that was a prospect he would have discarded, had he not listened to the entire message.

You might hear other valuable Smart information you can use, such as:

- An assistant's name and extension numbers.
- Others who may be able to help.
- Where the prospect is during his or her absence.
- What the prospect is doing.
- The pronunciation of his or her name if you don't know that already.
- When the prospect will return.

Have a pen in hand as you listen to their voice mail greetings so you can record this vital information.

Listen for Their Tone on Voice Mail

When you reach voice mail, pay particular attention to the decision makers' personalities on their greeting. This gives you some insight into the types of person they are and how you might approach them. If they sound rushed and quickly spit out their voice mail greeting, you know you should be prepared to be up-tempo and to-the-point when you reach them. You might hear someone who sounds very laid-back, warm, and welcoming; therefore, you would prepare to be a bit more informal on your call.

Put the Directions in Your Notes to Save Time

Some companies' voice mail systems seem to require a map just to get to your contact. You may occasionally need to trek through several layers of instructions before reaching your buyers; however, there are often simpler passages. Once you learn them, put the codes in your notes to save time: "Press # immediately, then 23 to get to Pat."

Opting Out to a Live Voice

When you prefer to speak with a real voice and not a digitized one upon reaching an electronic switchboard, you can try the standard escape hatches: hitting 0, *, or #. Another option is to simply stay on the line, since many systems revert to a live person if nothing is selected.

Use Your Prospect's Electronic System to Gather Intelligence

You can garner quite a bit of useful information about a company just by listening to its recordings. Scan the electronic options provided when voice mail answers. For example, when you're hit with an array of choices like "For Sales, press 2; for Service, press 3," listen to the various recordings, and return to the main menu to start over after each. You might pick up more information on what they sell and how, the size of the organization, how they service their customers, and other helpful clues. Additionally, if the voice mail system asks if you want to hear the directory, opt to do so. You might hear titles listed with names, or, if you already have written names, this can give you the correct pronunciations.

Call Back Immediately

After you leave a voice mail, try dialing right back. Think about it: How many times have you run for your ringing phone and just missed a call?

Call at Different Times of the Day

Make a note of what times during a day you miss your prospect and leave a voice mail. Try different times during the day. Best yet: Ask an assistant when your prospects are at their desks or when the best time to reach them is. For example, you don't want to keep bothering someone who isn't exactly a morning person at 8:30 AM every day.

Give Your Number Twice; Give Your Number Twice

One of life's little voice mail annoyances is having to play a message back to write down a phone number. So give yours twice. I like to say, "My number is 480-699-0958. I'll repeat that for you." And please, say it slowwwwwwwwwly. Another option is to give your number right at the beginning of the message, and then say you will repeat it at the end (but remember to do so!).

"Here's My Number . . ."

According to the *Amy Vanderbilt Complete Book of Etiquette* authors Nancy Tuckerman and Nancy Dunman, you should say, *"Here's my number,"* before you leave your phone number—and then pause for one or two seconds. It gives the person listening to your message a chance to retrieve a pen. Then pause every few digits, and repeat the number at the end so the person can check what she or he has written.

Smart Calling Tip

Write your phone number as you leave it on a voice mail message. This ensures you are saying it slowly enough for the person on the other end to write it as well.

Review Your Message, but Don't Assume You'll Always Have the Option

If you didn't feel as though you've left the perfect message in the way you wanted, many systems provide the option to hit a number to review it. While this is a good idea, don't make a day of it, and don't assume that you will *always* be able to do it. A sales rep told me his words turned to nonsense as he was leaving a message: *"And I'm calling about how we can, uh, create, uh, help to lower, um, er, your lower costs, I mean, ah hell, blah, blah, bladdy blah, oh screw it."* Then he hit #, thinking he would be able to rerecord the message.

Instead, he heard, *"Thank you. Your message has been delivered."*

Make Your Voice Mail Message Stand Out from the Clutter

Want to enhance the chances of your voice mail message being remembered?

- Back it up with a written message by an assistant. Ask the screener, assistant, or anyone in the area to scratch out a brief note for the prospect. For example, "Pat Walters left a voice mail regarding cutting maintenance expenses by 25 percent and will call back tomorrow."
- Ask them to *not* put it on your prospect's desk, but on his or her chair. That sets you apart.
- Further, ask them to draw a little smiley face next to the message. Don't laugh. Corny, to be sure, but memorable, right?
- Reinforce it with an e-mail, if you have—or can get—the address.

Of course, all of this must complement a great Possible Value Proposition. The message must be about your prospects and their world, what they want to achieve or wish to avoid. What we're doing with that message is making it stand out from the clutter.

Use a Last Resort Message

At some point of repeated futility—depending on their future potential and the size of your prospect pool—you need to punt and leave a final, firmer message. But when does that point come? If you sell office supplies, everyone could be a prospect, so the magic number at which you let go would be smaller than for someone selling train locomotives to railroads. What do you say?

> "I've tried several times to contact you about how we might be able to help cut your cost of customer acquisition by 20 percent like we have for B.O. Industries. If I don't hear back from you, I'm going to assume this is not something you'd like to discuss at this time."

This often elicits a response (I've even heard apologies) from people who are interested but were simply too busy to reply.

How One Rep's Message Prompted a Return Call

"I work in the software industry, specifically targeting printing companies. Although our sales cycle is usually around 60 days, we occasionally can sell on the spot, or it can take up to 3-plus years. I gave a demo of our product to a gentleman in Washington, D.C., and proceeded to follow up over the phone, as I am based in Lincoln, Nebraska. Every time I called, the gatekeeper would say the same line: "*I paged him twice, but he didn't answer.*"

It got so funny that I would mute my phone and put it on speaker for my colleagues to hear—because I could predict *exactly* what he would say each and every time. After multiple contacts—and the gatekeeper giving me the same line every time—this print shop finally got a voice messaging system. I may have been the first person ever to leave this man a voice mail, and it went something like this:

> "*Daniel, this is Greg from Digital IMS. This is my 48th attempt to get ahold of you after our demo. I will not be calling for you anymore. If you are interested in purchasing our product in the future, you can reach me toll-free at [toll-free number].*"

I left the file alone. Five weeks later, Daniel called me back and said, chuckling, "I was waiting for call number 50, but it never came—so I thought I should call you back."

He bought. It goes to show you that while persistence pays off, it's occasionally just as effective to let a prospect know that you are done investing time with them.

—Greg Daehling, Director of Sales, PrinterPresence by Digital IMS

Handling Unreturned Voice Mail Messages

Tom Mason, New Business Development Manager with Maclean Computing, has a great way to handle prospects who don't return the voice mail messages he leaves them. Here is an e-mail he sends:

> Dear Tyler,
> My name is Thomas Mason, and I work for a company called Maclean Computing Ltd. On the 5th of June, I spoke to Mark and he suggested that I speak to you regarding what we do here. I have tried to contact you since, on four

separate occasions. The dates for contact are the 11th of June, 20th of July, 23rd of July, and the 29th of July.

The reason for this e-mail is that I am concerned that I have done something wrong and that this is the reason why you are not returning my calls. Hence the title of my e-mail: "Advanced Apologies." If I have done something wrong, I would like to find out, so I can correct it. If you would like to talk to me, please give me a call at _____ or e-mail me at _____.

Thank you for your time.
Thomas Mason

After nine months of using this, Tom gets about a 90 percent hit rate, which is quite good in situations when most people would normally give up.

Shady Voice Mail Tactics to Avoid

As I mentioned in regard to the sleazy sales techniques some people teach and use regarding screeners, there are slimy voice mail methods you need to avoid. The first is simply leaving a message like this: "*Hi, it's Don Johnson. My number is 555-###-####. Please call me today.*"

That's it. No company name, no reason for the call. The rationale is that they must call you back since they have no idea why you called. In my case, I do have to call these people back. But when I quickly realize they are salespeople using a tactic to reach me, they had better have their A-game ready—since I usually skewer them.

This next one is just flat-out laughable, yet I've seen it suggested in print several times, been asked about it by participants in seminars, and have even run across a few people who claim to have used it.

"Hi, this is Pat Stone, at Halo Company. My phone number is 555-###-####. I have the most unbelievably great news for you. It's about . . ."

Then you hang up. That's right. *Hang up.* The reasoning behind this is that the people you're calling will be so interested in what you have to say that they will call you back. And then you are supposed to give the impression that you didn't know your message was cut off.

Give me a break. The end does not justify the means.

Smart Calling Action Steps

What will you commit to *do* as a result of this chapter?

CHAPTER

8

Working *with* Screeners, Gatekeepers, and Assistants?

Notice that I did *not* call this chapter "How to Get Past or Go around, over, through, or under Screeners and Gatekeepers." Yet that is precisely what much of the literature and instruction on the topic suggests.

What garbage that is!

I suggest the opposite. I could sum up my stance in a short sentence: *Treat the screener as you would the buyer.*

I personally don't like the monikers "screener" and "gatekeeper." They seem to imply something negative to me, almost as though it is their job to keep everyone *away* from the people you're attempting to contact. However, I'll use them here, since they are the common terms used to describe the people who protect decision makers.

First—just in case you have been or might be exposed to bad information about screeners—let's take a look at some of the nonsense that has been taught about screeners so we know what *not* to do. For example,

"Don't give them any information. They can't buy from you."

Wrong. Sometimes they can indeed buy from you, and often, they may influence a decision. The one thing they *can* do is make sure that *no one* will buy from you.

"*Answer their question abruptly, and make a demand of your own. As in 'I'm with AB Company. Will you connect me please?'*"

Oh, so that will intimidate them into putting you through? Right. People generally don't respond all that favorably to a rude demeanor.

"*Just tell them, 'It's a business matter that I need to speak with him personally about.'*"

You might as well say, "I'm a cheesy, self-important salesperson and I don't respect you."

"*If they get too nosy, say, 'Well, would Ms. Bigg approve of you denying her the opportunity to learn about what we have?'*"

Not only would she approve but also she would probably give the screener a raise.

I have to wonder if the people suggesting this stuff have ever actually placed a sales call. What do people who advocate such swill really think—that screeners are imbeciles? Wimps who allow themselves to be intimidated by such strong-arm tactics? In most cases, the screener is your *key* to the decision maker's door. That is, as long as you realize that he or she is not a barrier to be knifed through or steamrolled over. A person performing the role of a screener has one purpose in that job: to protect the decision maker's time. Your task, when necessary, is to help the screener realize you are important enough to earn an audience with the boss.

And don't you think screeners can instantly spot the shady tactics of callers who try to sleaze through? Please don't fool yourself. They're masters. And the more someone tries to scam them, the more firmly they bolt the air-tight door. Some screeners I've observed have hung up smugly, saying, "*There, take that you son-of-a-_____!*" Their perception of a caller's value diminishes in proportion to the elusiveness of the techniques used by the caller. And the higher up your decision maker is in an organization, the more skilled and experienced is the screener at reading the importance of sales callers, therefore compounding the reason to approach the screener as the professional that she or he is.

Gatekeeper Reality Check

"My wife is a receptionist, and what sales callers usually don't know is that she makes 90 percent of the purchasing decisions for the office, and there is only one person with authority over her (the CEO, her direct manager). She gets calls from salespeople who try to belittle her and get up to the decision maker and who don't realize that she is the decision maker and has more than just gatekeeper ability."

—Ryan Moore, Sales Rep, Chempoint

What to Do

Some prospecting systems and trainers will encourage you to spend as little time as possible talking to screeners. But doing so would cause you to miss opportunities to Smarten up your calls in the process. Think about it: This person is very close to the decision maker and has lots of valuable information. So work *with* him or her and attempt to establish a friendly rapport.

On a first call to a prospect, I suggest using the social engineering process discussed earlier.

1. Identify yourself and your company.
2. Ask for help.
3. Use a justification statement.
4. Ask questions.

Examples:

> "Hi, I'm Jason Andrews with National Systems. I hope you can help me. I'd like to speak with Ms. Peterson, and to be sure that what I'd discuss is most relevant, there are a couple of questions you could probably answer for me."

> "Hi, I'm Sandra Stone with Premier Software. I'm looking for some help. I want to be sure I'm in the right spot and I'd like to ask a few questions."

Then, simply begin asking.

Beginning this way sends the following messages to the screener:

- You're not like all of the other time-wasting salespeople who disregard the screener and try to bully or slime their way in.
- You actually are helping the screener do his or her job (by protecting the decision maker's time).
- The screener begins to form a relationship with you, which moves you closer to getting her or him to assist you.

Don't underestimate the importance of that last point. While doing research on a video program for getting to decision makers, I interviewed 50 screeners. In response to the question "How do you determine who gets put through?" the top answer was "People I like." A reader of my e-mail newsletter, Lisa Strong, wrote this to me:

> "I was an Executive Assistant to presidents and business owners of companies for years, and if you irritated me, you had zero chance of speaking with the owner. If I liked you, I would go out of my way to 'talk up' your company and made sure your correspondence was in his 'to read' file. Many times, when these owners were looking for new products or services, their Executive Assistants were responsible for doing the research and choosing the company that he should see. Therefore, treating whomever answers the phone with respect is in the salesperson's best interest."

Be Prepared to Sell the Screener If You Need to

There are those screeners who simply might be having a bad day. Perhaps they just spoke with a sleazy sales rep, and the resentment is still fresh, or maybe they just aren't very nice people. It happens.

If the screener asks what the call is about and needs a better reason than the one you provide to put you through—then be ready. I'll repeat that: You need to be prepared to matter-of-factly answer the screener's probing questions if they are posed, and your answers mustn't make her feel as though she's shadowboxing with you. They must leave her unequivocally fulfilled. She needs to be satisfied that you have something of value for her boss.

Think again about the screener's job. What happens when a less-than-ethical salesperson slithers through and wastes the decision maker's time? He cracks open his door, peeks out, and in an annoyed tone demands, "Why did you let that bozo through?" This accounts for the need to help her look good in her boss's eyes. So, when you get the "And what is this in reference to?" question, you need to respond—without hesitation—with your justification. For example, "*We specialize in helping parts manufacturers in your industry increase their short-term cash flow while they're waiting for their longer-term receivables to be paid. I want to ask him a few questions to determine how big of a problem this is for him, and see if it would be worth it for us to speak further.*"

At this point, if you haven't asked already, you might say, "*In fact, there's probably some information you could help me with.*" And as with voice mail, this answer should be very similar to the opening statement you will deliver to the buyer. Most important, *do not* discuss your product or service; talk about the results. It's very easy for a screener to say, "*We're* all set" or "We're happy with who we're buying from" when a salesperson mentions she wants to talk about postage meters. It's tougher to respond negatively when a rep says she has helped cut down other magazine publishers' costs of sending out their renewal statements and direct mail letters.

Smart Calling Exercise

Prepare your response to "What is this about?" (Again, you probably will want to wait until after the opening statement chapter, since your response will be a variation of the opening.)

Tips for Working with Screeners, Gatekeepers, and Assistants

Here are some tips you can use to be successful when working with screeners and assistants.

Use a Conversational, Yet Confident Tone of Voice

If you were standing in the lobby of their office, the screener would first size you up based on your appearance. They do the same with the way you sound, so don't sound sloppy or unimportant. However, you also want to avoid crossing the line into condescension or cockiness. You can sound confident without appearing pushy or demeaning.

Here are some weak words and phrases to avoid.

"Is Ms. Powell available, or is she busy?"

"Is Mr. Stevens in, or is he in a meeting?"

"May I speak with Donna, or is she doing something important?"

These questions minimize your status and make it easy to give you the brush-off.

Get the Screener's Name

Early in the conversation, ask for the screener's name. Use it on the call, put it in your notes, and greet the screener by name on the next call. You seem to be much less of a stranger on subsequent calls, and, of course, we all love the sound of our name.

Get Personal Information about the Buyer

After building rapport with the screener, the next step is to gather personal information about the boss: what hangs in the office, what personal items adorn the desk, personal interests, hobbies, or passions—in short, any valuable information that can help you begin a relationship.

Smart Calling Tip

A question we probably all hear on occasion is "Is this a sales call?" It typically comes from screeners looking to weed out sales reps who will just waste the boss's time. Here's a good response:

"I don't know yet. If there's a fit for what we have, it might be; otherwise, it's not. I specialize in working with IT managers, helping them reduce their workload and headaches regarding keeping track of the software they have installed on their machines. I'd like to ask Ms. Collins a few questions to see if we have the basis for further conversation."

Ask the Screener about the Decision Maker's Preferences

Don't hesitate to find out from screeners how the decision maker likes to be approached and addressed. For example, some people enjoy a little small talk; others prefer getting straight to the point. Some are offended when you use their first name too early in a relationship; others get uncomfortable when addressed as Mr. or Ms. You can also ask the all-important question: "Are there any topics I should avoid when speaking with her?"

Listen for the Names of Others

Any time the screener—or anyone—mentions the name of someone else in their organization, immediately jot it down. Then, when it is your turn to speak (do not interrupt), ask, "You mentioned 'Steve.' What does he do?" Also ask the screener who the boss reports to. This can help you learn the decision-making hierarchy, helping you ensure that you are talking to the appropriate people in the decision process.

When They Want You to Send Information

Just as it is when a prospect says, "Send some information on that," this might also be a screener's attempt to get you off the phone. Or it could legitimately be the way the prospect does business. I suggest you question to qualify the intent of the request: *"Actually, one of the purposes of my call is to see if it would be worthwhile to provide additional information. That's why I'd like to speak with him first: to determine what he might have interest in."*

In the cases where the screener says the decision maker always needs to see material first, be the professional that you are and agree to work with them. My good friend, a longtime columnist in my *Telephone Prospecting and Selling Report* newsletter, Jim Domanski has some fine tips on how to effectively work with screeners when sending information.

- **Address literature and other support material to the gatekeeper.** We sometimes have a tendency to address our support documents to the decision maker, even after we have begun working with the gatekeeper. In addition to the fact that this is demeaning to the gatekeeper, there's another reason to send material in this way: The gatekeeper rarely gets the same amount of mail that the decision maker receives. Therefore, a letter or package addressed to the gatekeeper is likely to be opened sooner.

- **Handwrite the address instead of using a typed label.** And if you can, put it in a plain envelope (rather than one with a company logo). Write your return address in the upper left corner, but do not include your own or your company's name. It's an old but still effective technique. There is a sense of mystery about a plain, handwritten letter or package. It gets opened first and is quickly remembered.

- **Make your support material pretty ugly.** The most important thing here is not to be visually appealing but rather to command the screener's attention. So use a highlighter on key areas. Write in the margins. Circle important things. Draw arrows to vital facts. Use Post-it flags if you have multiple-page documents. The gatekeeper is busy and is probably not an expert on your product or service. Make his job easier by giving him areas to focus on.

- **Forget the formal cover letter and use a Post-it note to accompany your material.** Ceremonial letters with stuffy words like "further to our conversation of September 30th, please find enclosed," well, stink, to be honest. Attach a sticky note with something like: "Shelly, here's a brochure on the projector. To make things a little easier for you, I have highlighted some key areas. Looking forward to talking with you on the 6th at 8:15."

It's plain, straightforward, nothing fancy or complicated. But note the clearly stated benefit for the screener (saves time) and the casual way that the telephone appointment is reinforced.

Reference the Pretty Ugly Brochure

In fact, you can use the actual words: *"Shelly, I'm following up on that brochure. It probably looked pretty ugly, but I wanted to save you some time."* If they opened it, they'll remember it—because it was unusual.

(*Jim Domanski is President of TeleConcepts Consulting, a telesales consulting and training firm. He's also the author of* Profiting by Phone *and* Add-on Selling. *See www.TeleConceptsConsulting.com.*)

Smart Calling Success Story

Sales rep Jim DeBender spends some of his sales time visiting customers. He always makes it a point to search out screeners and thank them for their help over the phone. You can just imagine how well received this gesture is. If you have the opportunity to visit customers or prospects, do the same.

Getting Your Messages to the Buyer

If the screener asks if you'd like to leave a message on voice mail, or if you have the option of having someone paged, respond with "How does she like to get messages?" This will improve your chance of more efficiently reaching the decision maker. Some people prefer to speak with the screener when they call in for messages and therefore attach more importance to the messages left with the screener. Some people simply hate to use their voice mail and may be lax in calling to check for messages. Again, a message left with the screener may yield better results. Conversely, the voice mail proponent might religiously retrieve messages. Either way, asking what's preferred could give you that slight edge.

Will You Help Me?

Another method for working with screeners—regardless of whether someone has voice mail—is to simply ask, "Will you have a chance to see Ms. Bigg when she comes back?" When they answer affirmatively, continue with "Great. When she picks up my message, would you please tell her personally that I really would like to speak with her today? I have an idea that she might want to know about." Because you're enlisting the screener's help—and acknowledging your awareness of his influence over the decision maker—you're endearing yourself to him a bit more while simultaneously emphasizing the importance of your message.

Go to the Highest Level

When in doubt about where you should start to locate a decision maker, find the level higher than the one that typically makes the decision for what you sell. The people here can give you good information. Typically, you will be referred down. Then at the next level, you can say, "I was speaking with Karen at Mr. McNabb's office, and she felt that Pat would be the person I should be speaking with." It's important that you don't imply that Mr. McNabb said that she should buy from you; just let them know that you've come from above, and your call will implicitly carry more clout.

For Buyers on Vacation

Find out as much as possible from the call screener about the decision maker's trip—especially when she's planning to return. It's probably not worth it to leave a message at this point, since she already has a big stack of mail, hundreds of e-mails, and 38 messages waiting for her when she returns, and your message will be number 26 in the middle of the stack. Instead, plan to call her when she returns, and give her a couple of days back in the office before you do so. If she returns on Monday, for example, you probably don't want to get in touch until Wednesday. Then, when you do call, you can ask about her vacation and use your interest in her trip as a basis for building rapport.

Smart Calling Action Steps

What will you commit to *do* as a result of this chapter?

CHAPTER
9

Opening Statements

What to Avoid to Minimize Resistance

It's show time. The curtain rises. The prospect has now answered the phone.

Don't screw it up.

I don't want to be negative, but the first 10 seconds is the time during which most prospecting calls die. They implode before leaving the starting gate. The good news is that failure is preventable and almost always a direct result of what the sales rep says.

To illustrate a point, here are two scenarios. Think about how you feel after reading each.

1. The remainder of this chapter will be about heating and air conditioning. We'll discuss all aspects of how buildings are heated and cooled. I have details of how heating and a/c units are wired and how ductwork is installed in buildings.

2. The remainder of this chapter is specifically about how you can get another week's worth of paid vacation this year.

What were your reactions?

After the first one, you were probably thinking, "I don't need to know this, and I don't want to hear about it. That's boring and does not affect me. I will extract myself from this situation." Conversely, after reading the second example, you were probably thinking, "That got my attention. I wonder what it is? Tell me more."

My point? In the first 10 seconds of phone calls, sales reps create the same emotions as those from my two scenarios. Therefore, you want to minimize or eliminate the feelings from the first scenario and strive for those that the second statement induces. We will begin our discussion of how to be successful with openings by reviewing the words, phrases, and questions I suggest you avoid—those that have a greater chance of evoking resistance than interest.

I have compiled this list based on more than 30 years of business-to-business experience, studying, listening, practicing, and tinkering with what works and what doesn't. As part of the customized training I provide companies, I review and fine-tune openings, and have done tens of thousands of them. And, where I have really honed my skills in this area is personally hearing lots of no's. Indeed, I have taken my beatings as a result of using many of these, so I am well-qualified to discuss them.

First, here are some key points about my "don't say" list:

- Some people can employ even the most ridiculous techniques—including these—and still show some success. It's usually attributable to their delivery and personality, but most other people would fail miserably with them.

- These suggestions are meant to minimize your chances for resistance. If something has a high probability for failure, why risk it?

- Nothing works *all* of the time. I've had people tell me, *"I've taken your suggestions, and they don't work for me."* Well, upon further examination in many cases, they weren't doing exactly as I suggested, or they were delivering it poorly, which contributed to the "not working." Again, my mantra: We want to maximize our chance for success, while minimizing the chance of failure. That's why I present these phrases to avoid.

Most people ashamedly admit, upon reading many of these examples, *"I say a bunch of those all the time."* That's okay, and part of the learning process. Again, I'm with you, since I, too, have made every mistake in the book. The key is learning from our mistakes, seeking and finding a better way, and moving on.

In the next chapter, we will look specifically at what *to* do in our openings. Right now, here is what you want to avoid.

What to Avoid Saying in the First 10 Seconds of Your Opening to Decision Makers

"Just" anything. The word *just* sounds weak and diminishes everything that follows it: "*I'm just calling to see if I could ask a few questions*" Just get rid of "just."

"Wanted to introduce myself and company to you." This isn't a cocktail party or a networking mixer. Remember who they care about: themselves, not you. It adds no significance and takes up valuable time.

Any mention of products or services without an accompanying results statement. As in, *"I'm with Dunlap Services, a local messenger service. I'd like to talk to you about your messenger needs."* In response, people can very easily say, *"We don't need that"* or *"We're satisfied with who we're using"* if you mention a product or service without the result. Products and services can incite resistance. Results are much tougher to reply negatively to.

"You sure are a hard guy to reach!" There's a good reason for this: They are busy and important. And you've just wasted a few seconds of their precious time stating the obvious. You've also positioned yourself as a salesperson and given them time to formulate their "I'm going to get this guy off the phone" strategy.

Sounding salesy.

This includes anything that reeks of old-school, smarmy, stereotypical salespeople. For instance:

"As you know, we are the top provider of. . . ." Whenever I hear "As you know," I begin thinking of reasons why I *wouldn't* know.

"I'm sure you would agree . . ." Tell people this, and they probably won't agree.

"If I could show you a way to get a top five position in the major search engines, you'd want that, wouldn't you?" Please, promise me you will never say, "If I could show you a way" in an opening. It is so absurd. You're asking someone to make a commitment before they know any of the details.

"Are you the person there in charge of. . . ?" As in *"Hi, I'm Pat Seller with ABC Company. Are you the person there who would handle the decisions regarding your_____?"* You might as well start off the call with *"I'm selling something. Are you the person I should be selling it to?"*

Someone reading this might ask, "Okay, but we *are* trying to sell something, and we want to be sure that this is the person we should be talking to, right?"

Right. But that *is not* the way or the time to do it, and we do not want it to seem like we are just trying to sell them something. Here's why:

- People would rather not talk to salespeople they don't know. It's natural, like the way we avoid the salespeople in retail stores who stalk after us and ask, *"May I help you?"* Again, people like to buy but don't want to be sold. A statement like this therefore announces your sales intentions, triggering the defensive posture.

- You have about seven seconds to move a person into a positive, receptive frame of mind on a Smart Call. If you're not doing that, they're slipping into a negative mind-set, moving into the "How do I get rid of this salesperson?" mode. The question about "Are you the person?" solidifies that before you have even begun to create interest.

- You should already know—*before* you ever hear their voice—that they are the decision maker for what you sell. You have read the previous chapters about gathering intelligence and social engineering, right?

"Can You Help Me?"

As we discussed in the chapter on gatekeepers and assistants, this is a valuable question with people performing those roles. With decision makers, however, it's a horrible technique. It creates resistance. Let's listen in:

Decision Maker (*interrupted from whatever she's doing—which is most likely not staring at the phone waiting for a sales call*): "*Pat Kelly here.*"

Caller: "*Hi Pat, Dale Doofus with Ace Services. Can you help me?*"

Decision Maker (*wondering "Who is this person, and what does he want? Probably a salesperson."*): "*What do you need?*"

Caller (*Now combining a couple of the other mistakes*): "*Yes, I was just wondering, are you the person there responsible for the secure storage of your paper records?*"

Decision Maker: "*I am, but we're all set.*"

Let's dissect what has happened: The caller wasted about 15 seconds arousing the decision maker's suspicion that he was probably someone calling to sell something and then confirming it. The negative momentum is like a freight train rolling downhill.

And by the way, her job is not to help you! How arrogant is that? Your job is to help *her!* You need to be able to *quickly* communicate how you might be able to do that before they have had a chance to move into "Get rid of salesperson" mode. Unless you're calling for a charity, don't call to ask for the decision maker's help.

Don't Apologize for Wanting to Help Them

Apologizing for taking someone's time at the beginning of a call diminishes your importance. For example, consider the caller who says, "*I know you're busy, and I'm sorry for interrupting. I'll take just a few seconds, and here's why I'm calling.*"

Stop. Think about what you're really offering. You have something of value that will help make this person's life better—right? If *you're* not sold on your importance, then *they* certainly won't be. *Everyone* is busy. If what you have is of value, you earn their time, and they'll want to speak with you. (More on the time issue later.)

"Thanks for Taking My Call"

There are very few instances in life where saying thanks does not make a situation better, and I maintain that the opening statement is one of those few. You can argue with me, but when a sales rep thanks me for taking his call, I hear: "*I feel like I'm not worthy of you, and I'm honored that a buyer would talk to me.*" It diminishes your importance in a buyer's mind. And it's another example of words taking up space and not adding value quickly.

Asking for a Decision, or Even Hinting at One

This is the error that has likely caused more calls to end abruptly than any other. Before I show it to you in a sales context, let's look at it in another perspective:

If a man approaches a woman he does not know in a bar and opens with *"Would you like to get married?"* he might get slapped or at least be viewed as a jerk.

Similar Questions

"I'd like to talk about beginning a relationship."

"I'm a real interesting guy and would like to set up a time for us to get together. Would 6:00 Friday be good?"

Ridiculous, cheesy, and a bit creepy.

Let's put it in a different context. A sales rep calls and opens with:

"I'd like to talk about becoming one of your vendors."

"I would like to talk about developing a relationship with your company."

"We have some great products and would like to come out there and discuss them with you. Would 3:00 Thursday be good?"

"I'm calling to invite you to a webinar next week."

Hmm, kind of puts it in perspective, doesn't it? Granted, all of those requests *could* be the end result, but it is far too early to ask for a decision, or even hint at one, in the opening.

Important point: When your call arrives, prospects are not in the preferred state of mind to hear a request for a decision, or even the insinuation that you are going to ask for a decision of any type. We must first *earn* the right to someone's time by piquing curiosity and quickly communicating some possible value. And we must keep earning it throughout our calls (and visits) to make appropriate recommendations when the time is right, and then secure commitments.

"I'm Calling People in Your Area" and "I Was Just Going Through My Records"

Oh, like that would make them feel special? They don't want to be treated as if they're just one of the names on the list you grabbed that day. People want to feel like they're the only person you're calling—not just one of the masses from a list of compiled names.

"I'm Updating My Database"
And why would they be inclined to help you do that?

"I'm Calling to Check in with You"
I jokingly refer to this as the probation officer approach. If you don't have something of value to offer, don't bother checking in.

"You and I Have Not Spoken Before"
That states the obvious; it's a waste of words.

"As You Can Guess, This Is a Sales Call"
You've got to be kidding me! It's as if the rep is saying, "Okay, I know I don't have a shot, and you're probably going to resist—but here goes."

"Just Wanted to Reach Out to You"
On top of the "just," what does reaching out mean—or do—for the listener?

The Baseball Opening
"Just wanted to touch base with you."
See the previous example's comments.

The "I've Got Too Much Time on My Hands" Call
"Thought I'd give you a call to see how it's going."
"Calling to see if you received the e-mail/letter/brochure/package/catalog/price list I sent."

Is the literature going to do the selling for you? If so, why are you needed? Granted, as we discussed, sending something can warm up a call, but do not ask if your prospects received it. It adds no value and, again, gives them time to move into a defensive frame of mind.

Show and Tell
Such as in "I want to *show* you how we could help you" or "I want to *tell* you how." Prospects interpret this as "Uh oh, sales pitch on the way. Raise the defense shields." Showing and telling insinuates a one-way communication, not the message we want to send.

"I'm _____ with _____. Are You Familiar with Us?"
If they aren't familiar with you, you'll have to explain your company anyway. It's not to your advantage to do it after they have said, "No, I'm not familiar." Plus, you haven't given them a reason to answer your questions

or to care about your company. If they answer that, yes, they are familiar with you, but they're not a customer, it leads to the beginning of a potentially uncomfortable situation, almost putting the person on the defensive. You do indeed want to find out what they know about you—later. Do not make that the focus of your opening statement. After you've generated some interest and curiosity with your brilliant opener, you can say, "By the way, so I'm not being redundant with my questioning, does our company name sound familiar at all to you?"

"I'm Not Trying to Sell You Anything"

Do sales reps who use this line think that their prospects are idiots who believe that? I feel that prospects look at sales reps who use that phrase as liars. Of *course*, our ultimate intent is to sell—we know it, and they know it. Furthermore, making a statement like this is a waste of time that could be better invested in moving the sales process forward while not alienating a prospect who sees through the deception. For users and defenders of this technique, save your e-mails; I don't want to see them. I've heard all the arguments for using this, such as it puts the other person at ease, it lets them know you're not going to give them a pitch, and it positions you as more of an information-gatherer instead of a one-call closer salesperson.

Whatever.

We're going to accomplish the same thing with our interest-creating opening without wasting words. If you begin calls by saying you're not going to sell anything, then that will usually be your end result.

"Do You Have a Few Minutes to Talk?"

Let me clarify this one, since there are some exceptions. What I suggest you avoid is this:

Prospect: "Stan Jablonski."

Sales Rep: "Hi, Stan. Andy Koval with Thurston Packaging. Do you have a minute?"

Let me ask you: If you were a decision maker who received a call like this, what would go through your mind? You don't recognize this person or company, you are up to your neck in your work and just happened to pick up the interrupting ringing phone, and you're asked if you have a minute? The typical reaction is "Not really" or "Quick, what do you have?" Not the frame of mind we want them in.

This does not suggest, however, that you shouldn't respect their time. How you do so is a matter of your personal choice; however, this approach isn't it. As with some of the other phrases to avoid, I have the better alternative in the next chapter.

Being Assumptive in the Opening and Using Declarative Statements

Do not tell prospects what you *will* do in your opening. Don't tell them that you *can* save them money. Do not state that you *will* help them increase sales. Avoid saying that they *will* lower their costs and increase their profits.

What?

Am I stark-raving, lost-my-sales-mind crazy?

No. You want to avoid using definitive, declarative statements in the first few sentences of your calls. Why? Because even though you probably do believe you could make them money, save them money, or cut costs, and you probably could, what's important is that *they* might not believe that. All of those statements make the assumption that something is wrong with their business or company. Again, maybe something is, but let's turn the tables. Put yourself on the receiving end of this: If someone you don't know or respect gives you unsolicited advice and tells you that you're doing something wrong, what's your response? Naturally, you resent it and become defensive. The same is true on the phone with prospects; they don't want to hear your assumptions about the problems in their organization. If you make those kinds of bold statements early— before they have bought into the concept that you might indeed be able to deliver some value—you run the risk of creating resistance.

For example, take this opening: "*Mr. Prospect, we are a credit card processing company and can save you money on your card processing fees.*" Let's say the prospect has invested lots of time in studying the various alternatives for card processing, tested a few different companies, and maybe even presented a seminar on how to select the best processor at his industry's national conference. If he gets cold-called and hears a sales rep make this definitive statement, here's what's probably going through his mind: "Who is this bozo, and how can he make that claim without knowing anything about me? I'm getting rid of him." He's not ready to hear such a bold statement yet, is likely to doubt its validity, and might even be offended by it.

The dilemma here is that we *do* want them thinking about the possible value we will hint at, and we want them to feel that since there might be some truth to what we say, they want to hear more. That's why later I'm going to show you how to soften your claim in your Possible Value Proposition in the opening by using weasel words. (Don't be alarmed—they are much better than the title suggests!)

Reacting to Unusual Names

Dale Carnegie is credited with saying that the sweetest sound a person can hear is his own name.

It's true, for the most part—when used appropriately by the right person at the right time. Conversely, in some cases, a person's name can be a turn-off.

I am still floored by people's ignorance in regard to hearing a difficult-to-pronounce or unusual name on phone calls. In talking to sales or service people on calls where I was the customer, after spelling my name, I've heard such idiotic comments as:

"Oh, that's a weird one."

"That's a strange name."

And some people just burst out laughing. What do these dolts think? That I'm going to say, "Yeah, I know"? I personally don't stay up nights fretting over this; mine *is* an unusual name. (It's pronounced Sob'-check.) I'm used to it. Hey, to top it off, my first name is Art. Think of how many times I heard "Art Fart" while growing up, or "I bet Art is your favorite Sub-JECT (yuck yuck)." People can be such morons.

But the name issue is a very tender area for some people, and it says a lot about the person making the comment. I don't mind if, after saying or spelling my name, a fellow Pole makes a commiserating comment like *"I've got you beat. My name is Wojtkewkowski."* Otherwise, it's really out of place to make inappropriate comments.

If someone with an unusual name takes the lead and pokes fun at it himself after spelling it, it's certainly okay to react in some way. I make a point to spell my name, SO-BC-ZAK. Then I say, "I used to start out with 'SOB,' but too many people commented on how descriptive that was." That breaks the ice and elicits some laughter and small talk. The safe rule: Absent their self-deprecating comment, say . . . nothing.

I once took a call from a guy who recited very slowly his name: *"Buddy Bunne."* And he pronounced it BUN-EE, like a little rabbit (but he didn't say that). I admit, I bit my lip and paused, and you could almost feel him bracing for the wise guy response. *"And your address, Buddy?"* I continued.

Pssst: Here's a secret. People with unusual names *know* their name is different. Some good-natured folks just blow off comments with humor. But others view their name as sensitively as they would if they had a third ear protruding from their head. You wouldn't comment on that, so why take a chance of offending someone?

Smart Calling Tips

1. Here's a website where you can enter names and hear an audio with the pronunciation: www.pronouncenames.com/. You can also add pronunciations that you know to be correct, and perhaps variations of others.
2. Before reaching the prospect, ask someone at the prospect's company how to pronounce the name. (And please, do *not* say, "What is the *correct* pronunciation of Bill's name?" Like you are looking for the *incorrect* way to say it?)
3. Also ask others how the prospect prefers to be addressed: Robert, Bob, Mr. Smith, and so on.
4. Do not rename them. Use their name the way it is written and the way they say it when they greet you. For example, one of my customers, David, said that people often call him Dave even after he answers the phone with "This is David."

How Are You Today? Use It or Not?

A sales rep called me and said, *"Hi, this is Jane Davis with Technology Associates. How are you doing today?"*

"Jane, I'm just doing fantastic," I replied.

She jumped back in as the last syllable was leaving my lips: *"I'm doing fine, thank you, the reason I'm calling is . . ."*

What? Did I miss something? I almost laughed out loud.

Of course, I really didn't pay attention to anything else she said. (From what I recall, it wasn't interesting anyway—not surprisingly.)

This topic certainly isn't one of a high-level sales process nature; however, I do find that it stimulates lots of interest and discussion in seminars. My friend and fellow author-trainer Jim Domanski first referred to it as the HAYT question: "How are you today?"

Here's my official stance on the issue of small talk at the beginning of the call:

- **Use it if you are comfortable.** Informal surveys in training workshops consistently show that 30 percent of you are all for using it, 30 percent wouldn't use it unless forced to at gunpoint, and 40 percent will use it based on the situation. It depends on your personality and preference. I've heard reps who could use it with the gruffest of prospects and turn them into melted butter. There are others who are so against its use that they could never get a positive response since it sounds forced when they try it. Personally, I'll use it when I get good mojo at the other end of the phone. If they sound like the type of person who will react favorably, I let it fly.

- **Use something different.** Let's face it: "How are you today?" is pretty much a throwaway question. Its main purpose is to break the ice and ease some tension. It's customary. If you were in a prospect's office, there would be the obligatory comments about the photos on the desk and the moose head on the wall. But the phone is a more formal communication medium; therefore, it's not as easy to insert small talk. That doesn't diminish the need for it or its possible positive effect—or the negative, for that matter, like the previous example.

So, I suggest saying something different to avoid sounding like every other caller. For example,

> "How's your Tuesday so far?"
>
> "How's the day treating you?"

Or, TELL them they are having a good day:

"You sound like you're having a good day?"

"Hi Mary, sounds like you are having a good Thursday . . . I'm looking for David please . . ."

"Mike, hope you're morning is going well . . . I'm Pat Seller . . ."

"Good morning Dale, hope you are doing great . . . I'm Karen Davis . . ."

Full disclosure here: I had a client where the reps would be brutally honest based on what they heard in the other person's voice when they answered, even if it was negative. For example,

"Kathy, sounds like things are not going your way this morning."

I almost leaped out of my chair when I first heard that. But the more calls I heard, the more I realized that people reacted and started talking, giving information about themselves. Not sure still if I am ready to try it, but I'm just reporting what I observed.

- **Put feeling in it.** You can easily spot the "How are you today?" that is monotone and mechanical, and it does more harm than good. Your tone of voice makes the difference. Keep this in mind: People often place more meaning on your tone than on your words. Ask the question as if you mean it!

- **Listen to the answer, and react accordingly.** Obviously, the rep in my example wasn't listening to my response. She expected a certain answer, waited until I finished making sounds (almost), and then continued with what she was conditioned to say regardless of my response. An argument against using any type of HAYT question is that the people on the other end of the line might tell you how exactly how badly their day is going. Fine—then react and ask them about it. Empathize. At least you're in a conversation now. And you're listening to them.

- Use the HAYT question if you are comfortable doing so, but please keep these ideas in mind.

Smart Calling Action Step

What will you commit to *do* as a result of this chapter?

Creating Interest with Your Smart Call Opening Statement

Now that I have trashed almost everything that you might have been taught about what to say on a prospecting call, I guess it's time for me to step up to the plate with what you *should* do. And I will; you won't be disappointed.

In fact, if you read only one chapter in this book—which I hope you don't do—this one would be worth many times more than your investment in the entire book. We are about to cover the step-by-step process for pulling everything together that we have covered so far—all of your planning and your intelligence gathering—and plugging it into your interest-creating opening statement.

The Jim Furyk Theory

I must preface everything I suggest about openings with what I call the Jim Furyk Theory. Jim is a PGA golfer, and if you follow golf, you have undoubtedly seen him play. What makes Furyk unique is that he has one of the more unconventional swings in golf. Okay, some say it looks a bit odd. All right, I won't mince words; it's just plain ugly. However, Jim is one of the best golfers in the world; he's won a major championship and many tournaments. There probably is not a golf teacher alive, though, who would ever teach a golf swing the way Furyk executes it. But what they do teach—and agree upon—is that the club head needs to be square to the ball at impact to realize the optimal result. While Jim Furyk's golf swing itself—what happens before he hits the ball—is ugly, he squares the club at impact, and his results prove it.

The correlation for us as Smart Callers is that I do not claim to have the one and only perfect opening statement methodology for prospecting. My goal is to help you to maximize your chance of squaring the club head at impact to get the result you desire, while minimizing the results to avoid—resistance.

Sure, I've given you a number of "don't say" phrases, and I am about to show you many more "to do's" for your openings. These are based on what I know to work from experience, study, and implementation—my own, and thousands of salespeople I have worked with. I also know that there are probably some Jim Furyks out there who can show some success using unconventional techniques, and there are a number of ways to get the club head square or the results we desire. That's why I will present to you a number of options, and it will be your responsibility to mold, shape, and beat these into a form that works for you.

Two Objectives for Your Openings

Let's first be clear on what you're trying to do with openings. You have two simple objectives for your opening statement:

1. To move your prospects into a positive, receptive frame of mind to participate.
2. To move them to the questioning phase of the call and begin to get them talking.

That's it. As we discussed in the last chapter, you don't want to give a presentation, ask for a decision or appointment, or talk about products or services. You just want them to be curious, interested, and talking.

Scripting

The worst time to think of what you'll say is when it's already leaving your mouth. *Scripts.* Just saying the word causes many professionals to crinkle their noses with disdain and screech, "Scripts, no way! They're not natural, they make you sound canned!" On the contrary, not using a script often makes you sound like a moron, and failing to prepare a script for your opening and voice mail message is just plain dumb.

As for the claim that a script makes you sound canned, well, have you been to a movie or watched a TV series lately? This might come as a shock, but they were all working from scripts. Someone wrote those words they're saying *for* them. Scripts don't make you sound canned; the *delivery* of a poorly constructed script can make someone sound canned.

I define a *script* as the conversational combination of well-planned words that, when delivered naturally, elicit the listener response we desire. Dissenters who say they just like to wing it on the phone cause me to shake my head in disbelief, because winging it often results in a rambling, stream-of-consciousness monologue that *never* will be better than something prepared in advance.

Let's put it in a different perspective and pretend that you were asked to write an article for the highest-profile trade publication in your industry. This article could give you celebrity status and maybe even cause prospects to view you as *the* expert in the business with whom they want to work. It could be a career-defining article. Would you scratch out the first thing that came to mind and submit your rough draft to the publication's editor? *No!* You'd give it some thought, do some research, prepare an outline, do a first version, edit it, maybe have someone else look at it, revise it, and continue the process until you had something very tight that you were comfortable with. Why? Because you'd want it to be the best it could possibly be.

Now, let me ask you, if a sales rep dials the phone—completely scriptless—and blurts out the first thing that comes to mind, just winging it, what is he submitting? It is essentially a rough draft, which, of course, is nowhere near the quality of something he might take the time to *prepare*.

Organizing what you'll say in advance of the conversation allows you to fine-tune and economize the precise combination of words that will give you the result you're looking for. The key to sounding smooth is in writing it in a conversational tone and then delivering it naturally. And just like an actor, that requires studying and practicing it.

The Smart Call Interest-Creating Opening Statement Process

It's time to pull everything together with the step-by-step opening statement process. Here's how:

1. Introduce yourself and your organization.

    "Hi_____, I'm_____ with_____."

    Easy so far.

2. Use your Smart Call intelligence.

    Here, you employ something you know that implies you are not the typical cold caller, the more tailored and on-target, the better.

    "I was speaking with_____ and she mentioned that you are now in the process of_____."

    "Congratulations on the_____ I had read about in_____."

    "I've been following your Twitter conversation about___"

    "My compliments on the article you posted in the Java Developers group on LinkedIn."

    "I see that your firm is now going to_____."

    "I understand that one of your major initiatives for the year is_____."

    "At your website I had seen_____."

3. Hint at your Possible Value Proposition.

    You want to tailor your PVP to their world, further tying together everything else we've covered.

    "We specialize in working with_____, in helping them to deal with the issue of_____."

    "In working with other_____, we have been able to help them_____."

    "It sounds like you might be experiencing_____. If so, we have provided solutions that help to_____."

    "With other_____ in the same situation, we have been able to_____."

4. Suggest more possible value, contingent on moving to questioning.

    This is the step where you build on your PVP and begin to ask questions specifically tailored to their responses, situations, and questions of you.

    "I've got a few ideas that might be of some value to you regarding _____, and I'd like to ask a few questions."

"We might have a few options that could possibly be a fit for you as well. If I've reached you at a good time, I'd like to ask a few questions to see if I could provide you with some information."

"We've been able to repeat these results with over 220 companies, and with a few questions we could determine if it would be worth it for you to take a look at some information."

"Depending on where you are in your selection process, we might have some options worth taking a look at."

More Possible Ending Phrases

". . . see if we should talk further."

". . . determine if it's something you'd like to take a look at."

". . . find out if it might be of some value to you."

". . . see if it might be an option worth considering."

Let's look at some full examples, using some of the Possible Value Propositions I had referred to in Chapter 3.

"Hi, Dr. Moeller, I'm Stephen Drury with Smile Marketing. I noticed the coupons you are running in the school paper and spoke with your office manager about some of the marketing you are doing to build your practice. We have helped other pediatric dentists cut their cost of new patient acquisition by an average of 50 percent while increasing their number of new patients by 25 percent within six months. Depending on what your goals are, we might have a few options worth taking a look at."

"Dan, I'm Karen Browning with Integrated Software. I was at your website and downloaded your report from the new book on managed health care. In speaking with Kelly, your marketing assistant, I understand that you're exploring options to streamline the steps it takes to do your online follow-up with those types of leads. We've had a few other publishing clients who were using 5 to 10 different programs to manage the various aspects of their online marketing and sales. We've managed to replace all of these programs with just one, cutting their software costs, saving hours of time, and in some cases, doubling their online book sales. I'd like to ask a few questions to see if this might be something worth taking a look at."

"Heather, I'm Kyle Johnston with Personnel Solutions. I saw your Twitter posting mentioning how many unqualified applications you had to go through the other day. We specialize in reaching high-level managers in your industry who otherwise might not be looking for positions. Recruiters who use our career postings tell us that the candidates they attract are better-qualified—which saves them hours per week by not having to deal with applicants who would never be considered."

"Hi, Jack, I'm Zack Krandle with Hometown Construction. In reviewing some of the reports from the city permits department, I came across some of the properties that your firm manages. We have a good relationship with the inspectors here in town; we know their tendencies and specialize in working with landlords whose properties failed building inspections and fix them so they pass. If this is a good time, I'd like to ask a few questions."

Here are a few more:

"In reading your company blog, I saw that there have been some challenges with customer deliveries over the past few months. We specialize in working with businesses that ship with UPS, FedEx, and DHL, helping them take advantage of the guaranteed refunds the carriers offer for late delivery. We've been able to help most of our clients get refunds ranging from a few hundred to thousands of dollars per year, depending on shipping volumes. If I've reached you at a good time, I'd like to ask a few questions to see if it would be worth our while to talk further."

"Mr. Prospect, I'm_____ with_____. I was speaking with your business manager and understand that a growing part of your noninsurance business is paid by credit card—and you've recently had your transaction fees raised. We've worked with a number of auto repair shops and helped them cut some obscure credit card processing fees they weren't even aware they were paying—thereby allowing them to keep a greater percentage of every ticket. We might be able to do the same for you; I'd like to ask a few questions to see if I could provide you more information."

Does Length Matter?

I'm often asked about the proper length of an opening, how long is too long, and the like. As a general rule, you want to say as much as you can with the fewest number of words—which means that *every word* should add to the impact of the opening. If words don't, edit them out.

I know from experience that some people might look at the opening examples here and say, "Too long!" My response is that something is too long only if it is delivered poorly and doesn't interest the listener. If your opening is laser-targeted to the prospect's world, she will listen. Conversely, if it is irrelevant, even one sentence is too long in his mind.

The Time Issue

As I mentioned in the previous chapter, you might want to verbalize respect for prospects' time. I can understand that. Some people want to do it all of the time, while others think that it provides an opportunity for the prospect to say, "I'm too busy to talk." Since I can argue both sides of that issue, I suggest that its use is purely a matter of personal preference. My one rule, however, is to *not* simply say: "Do you have a few moments to talk?" right at the beginning (as I pointed out in the previous chapter). If you do want to mention time, I always recommend that you do so *after* making your Possible Value Proposition. Notice that in one of the examples of my formula, I use the phrase "and if I have reached you at a good time." That is not a question but a statement, one that's strategically positioned after the value to give the prospect a reason to stay on the phone. If they are so busy right now that they can't speak with us, they'll let us know (actually, they probably wouldn't have picked up the phone in the first place if they were *that* busy). Otherwise, it's embedded in the sentence where we suggest that we'd like to ask a few questions.

An Unconventional Technique That I Have Heard Work

As part of my preparation for customized training programs for companies, I like to listen to their recorded calls. On the first few calls with one particular client, I heard the rep introduce himself and his organization and then say, "I'll be brief, if that's okay with you." My first reaction was negative, thinking that was a bit cheesy. Then I heard the rep use it on almost every call, and not one prospect responded, "No, please, be as verbose as you can." Everyone responded with something like "Sure, go ahead." This may not be for everyone, but it is an option I'll put in the Jim Furyk category.

Weasel Words

You might have also noticed I used a number of words that are not typically associated with strong sales language. They might actually seem weak, but that's by design. I do suggest using some weasel or contingency words like:

Might

Maybe

Perhaps

Depending on

In Chapter 9, I advised against using declarative statements. We use these weasel words instead, because we want to avoid having prospects see us as that pushy, cocky salesperson. These words soften up the opening, and help us transition into the questions:

". . . and depending on your satisfaction with the speed and downtime of your Internet connection, we might be able to help you cut down on the time you spend waiting for pages to load, and minimize those interruptions in service your assistant said you are experiencing. . . ."

And notice how this leads right into questioning.

". . . and if I've caught you at a good time, I'd like to ask a few questions . . ."

Smart Calling Tip

If a prospect answers the phone and sounds hurried, don't let that scare you into rushing your opening or questioning. Some people naturally speak in a fast-paced manner, and others do it with salespeople until the rep builds rapport.

You Have Also Created Your Smart Voice Mail Message

As we've discussed, your opening statement does double duty as your voice mail message to the prospect. The only difference is the ending. I'll modify one of the openings I shared previously into a voice mail message:

"Hi, Jack, I'm Zack Krandle with Hometown Construction. In reviewing some of the reports from the city permits department, I had seen some of the properties that your firm manages. We have a good relationship with the inspectors here in town; we know their tendencies and specialize in working with landlords whose properties failed building inspections and fix them so they pass. I'd like to ask a few questions to see if I could provide you some information. I will call you again Friday morning, and if you'd like to call me before then, my number is. . . ."

Smart Calling Exercise

Write out your own opening statement. Using one of the prospects for whom you have already done your intelligence gathering and some social engineering, create a customized, tailored opening. Then edit it, and share it with a fellow sales rep for input.

Smart Calling Action Step

What will you commit to *do* as a result of this chapter?

Handling Early Resistance on Your Smart Calls

Reality check: Even if you do *everything* I've suggested so far, point-by-point perfectly, you will still get people who respond with some variation of "I'm not interested" or "We're happy with what we're doing."

Expect it. Don't be deterred by it. And prepare for it. That's what we'll do in this chapter.

Resistance after hearing an opening statement from an unknown caller is a natural, conditioned reaction for many people. And it usually works in attempts to blow sales reps off the phone. Except you, of course, because you'll have some conversational ways to get the prospect talking, which really is the key to keeping the call alive and creating an opportunity.

I have a name for these kinds of inherent reactions that sales calls tend to elicit from prospects: Resistant Reflex Responses (RRRs). They simply are a natural reflex for many people, like ducking if an object is flying at your head. It's instinctive. Not much thought goes into them; they just happen.

Trying to counter them with logic is tough, since, well—what would you be arguing against? We haven't heard anything of substance yet, other than the response. And you don't want to use a goofy retort that some sales books suggest: "Well, of course you aren't interested—I haven't given you anything to be interested in yet!" Give me a break.

So what should you do? Get them talking—which moves their mind away from their reflexive response and on to something of substance.

Use a Pattern Interrupt

A model of communication called neurolinguistic programming that was popularized by many self-help gurus (most notably Tony Robbins) over the past 20 years espouses a theory and technique called a pattern interrupt. Without causing your eyes to glaze over in boredom, let me simplify it for our purposes: When people do or say something automatically, it's called a pattern. If you do something that stops that pattern and gets them talking or thinking about something else, then that is a pattern interrupt. In what city were you born?

That last question was a pattern interrupt. You were reading along, and I interrupted you with a question that probably caused you to think about the answer (or wonder if I had gone off the deep end). Either way, using a pattern interrupt when you hear a Resistant Reflex Response causes someone to answer a question. For example:

Prospect: *"I'm not interested."*
Sales rep: *"I see. Where are you now getting your compressors?"*

Here's another:

Prospect: *"We're all set."*
Sales rep: *"I understand. When is your next project coming up?"*

One more

Prospect: *"We wouldn't need that."*
Sales rep: *"Oh. How are you now handling written-off receivables?"*

This is not difficult to execute. You simply need to anticipate the RRRs you are likely to hear, or if you have placed calls for more than a day, you already know which ones you hear. Then you prepare your response.

Your tone plays a vital role in determining the success of your reply. Use a soft, almost surprised—maybe even disappointed—tone of voice. By no means do you want to seem confrontational. We want them to open up and drop their shield—not feel threatened.

You might think that you're likely to hear something like "Look, what part of 'I'm not interested' do you not understand?" after your response, and you would be right. This certainly won't work every time; nothing does. However, you may at least be able to salvage some opportunities that you would not have gotten otherwise—possible sales you can cash in on either now or in the future. Your return on your minuscule time investment is huge, and you have nothing to lose.

The Softening Statement

You might have noticed that before asking the question in each of the examples, I used a few words such as "Oh," "I see," and "I understand" to diffuse tension and soften the question. I suggest you do the same. Fellow sales trainer and founder of the prospecting system Unlock the Game Ari Galper suggests a great softening statement: *"That's not a problem."* Then he recommends diffusing the tension with something like *"I'm not trying to replace your current vendor. Would you be open to some different ideas that you might not be using now?"*

It's So Simple Even a Fourth-Grader Can Do It

I attended a fund-raising dinner as part of a celebrity golf tournament for Arizona youth baseball. Got to meet a few Hall of Fame Major League baseball players—very cool.

During the dinner, kids were working the crowd selling raffle tickets. I had already purchased five $20 tickets earlier at the door, and a fourth grader (as I later found out) approached our table and very confidently asked, "Would you like to buy some raffle tickets?"

I smiled and told her I already had bought mine. I was impressed that these kids were approaching adults and asking for money (although I'm sure they do it to their parents all the time), so I tried to be as gentle as possible in saying no: *"Oh, no thanks. I already bought some."*

She looked at me with these beautiful blue eyes, smiled, and in a soft tone replied:

"That's okay."

I didn't know what to say. She totally disarmed me.

"You didn't get any from me yet."

I had nothing! Brilliant! *Of course* I had to buy more. That's a great example of someone not being deterred by an initial no, and in fact being prepared for it, and then asking again.

I actually had no good reason for not buying another one—it was a fund-raising event, after all.

Smart Calling Exercise

Write out the Resistant Reflect Responses you regularly hear and/or anticipate. For each one, develop your softening statement and question. Then, practice reciting them out loud or, even better, role-play them with a partner.

Here's the One Place Where Sounding Dumb Works

After your opening you might hear some resistance with reasoning that just doesn't make sense. So react accordingly. Act confused. For example:

> Prospect: "Yeah, I've heard of you guys before. It just wouldn't be right for us."
>
> Sales rep: "I'm not following. Could you explain?"

We want them to continue talking, since the more they say, the less their initial resistance will make sense—and the more you will have to work with. Other examples include:

> "Mr. Davis, I'm not sure I fully understood what you just said. Will you please repeat that for me?"
>
> "Pat, I heard what you said, but I'm not following the reasoning. Would you mind explaining it for me?"

Responding When They Are Happy with Their Present Supplier

Here are a few suggestions from sales reps and managers on how to handle variations of "We're happy with our present supplier," when heard at the beginning of a prospecting call.

Sales manager Ben Hyman has his reps say,

> *"That's fine, Mr. Prospect; we realize that you're most likely satisfied at the current time. We would still like to keep in touch as we provide information and education to those companies that are a good fit for our technology. We are producing some webinars and white papers on the newest supply chain solutions—would you like to receive them?"*

If they say yes, we then say,

> *"Great! May I ask you just a few questions so that when we send you information, it will be tailored to your organization?"*

Ben says that this often results in receiving numerous calls from companies wanting to receive more info and several that want to look at his offerings because they are *not* satisfied with their current provider.

Sales pro Evonne Weinhaus suggests saying,

> *"Teach me if you would, what kind of (service, product, things) would it take for you to feel better than satisfied?"*

If they have trouble answering the question at first, that is okay. You can restate your point and use different words. Just make sure you recognize what you are accomplishing by asking this one simple question:

- You put the notion of "I'm satisfied" in a totally new framework. It is now positioned as second best, *without* you trying to prove that point.
- By using the phase, "teach me," you switch the balance of power. They are in the driver's seat teaching you, and you are learning from them.

Rick Kendall, a sales rep with Branom Instrument Company, says that he requests a chance to quote his comparative product anyway—just to make sure that prospects are getting the most value for their money. They very rarely refuse a quote. He then gets into the call where he would not have otherwise, and quite often he wins a sale since his quotes are very competitive.

Inside sales rep Jeff Wirsing responds, *"That's fine, Mr. Client. In the event that something changes with your current service/supplier, would it be all right if I stay in touch?"* Then he questions what would need to change, placing him into a sales conversation.

Michael Bechtel, of D&H Distributing, said,

"In my industry, there tends to be a lot of shortages, especially in the newest of the products. I like to find something that the prospect uses that I know is hard to find—say, a hot new video card, for example—and then ask if he ever has problems getting that item. When he says yes, I mention that if nothing else, I would love to be his second source. After all, who wants to rely on one person only for their products during an allocations period? I like to always start off with the second source method; it sounds like you aren't trying to break up their current relationships with other vendors."

Jared Olson, a sales pro with General Service Bureau Inc., says,

"When someone tells me they are 'happy with their present set-up,' I respect that answer and simply follow up with 'How often or when will you next evaluate the present set-up?' Depending on the answer I receive, I will follow up with 'Under what circumstances would you consider switching your present set-up?' (Which I believe was in your books.) If they open up and questioning can continue, I do so. However, I can usually get at least those two questions answered—which helps me figure out when I should call back again. I deal primarily with CFOs, so I want to be respectful of their answer when they tell me that they're currently happy."

How to Answer "Send Me Some Literature on That"

If this statement occurs later in the call, it might be a legitimate request—and indeed be worth your while to send information. (I have an entire article on this topic that helps you determine when it is worthwhile. To access the information free, go to www.Business ByPhone.com/literature.htm.) However, when the literature request occurs early in a call, it often is an attempt at a brush-off. You want to try to move to the questioning. Reply with *"I'll be happy to provide you with some information. So that I can tailor it for your situation I'd like to ask a few questions."*

"Why Should I Consider You?"

Here's a trap that prospects sometimes set and sales reps walk right into. After the opening, the prospect says something like "Why should I use your company?" The wrong answer is to actually name your reasons, which simply provides them with more reasons to get you off the phone. Instead, you want to move to the questioning. Here are possible responses:

> *"There might be a few reasons. I'll need to find out more about your situation before I'm sure."*
>
> *"That's the reason for my call: to find out specifically how we could help. I'll need to ask you a few questions to learn more about."*

Responding When They Try to Rush You

You might sometimes hear something like "Okay, you've got two minutes." Here are three suggestions:

1. *Do not become flustered.* You'll spill your entire presentation as fast as it can be sprayed from your lips. This is a tactic some prospects use to rattle salespeople.
2. *Ignore the time limit.* Assuming you have captured and maintained their interest, they will also forget what they said about time.
3. This contradicts the previous suggestion, but it also can work: *Address the time factor immediately.* "I'll be happy to call back when you have more time, since there are several details I need to learn about your situation before I can determine how much we could save you."

Simple Response to a Quick "Not Interested"

Here's a simple, effective way to reply to an immediate "Not interested": *"Does that mean never, or just not now?"* This often keeps the conversation and the door open with prospects who admit that situations could change.

Handling the Early Price Question

Once you've given your opening statement, the response you might hear is *"What does it cost?"*

You do not want to involve yourself in a price discussion before you've asked any questions, identified needs, and identified the specific value you could deliver. Therefore, you want to defer answering, while giving them some satisfaction. For example:

> "It depends on several variables. Let me ask you a few questions so I can quote you the best price for your situation."

If they insist, "Just give me the price," you could try

> "Well, it could be as low as $_____, or up to $_____. Let's take a look at your situation."

Or

> "I imagine you want the best price, right? To determine that, we'll need to take a look at your situation."

Early Resistance Case Study

Question

Art, I work at a company that sells its own line of safety glasses. I recently had called on a big industrial supply catalog company with the objective of getting our products into their catalog. The response I immediately received—and commonly get from companies with catalogs like that—was "At this time, we are not looking for additional safety eyewear suppliers." How would you personally handle this kind of response? Or how would you set yourself up for future contact with this company? Would you send a follow-up letter to them?
> **—Thanks for any helpful insight,**
> **Gary Gabrielse, Global Vision Eyewear**

Answer

Gary, most buyers are not actively looking for something different from what they have. Therefore, your strategy should be asking questions like:

- *"For future reference, what is the process for evaluating new products?"*
- *"Who is involved"*? (This is important since it's probably not just one person.)
- *"What are the decision-making criteria?"*
- *"How did they choose what they use now?"*
- *"Under what circumstances might they look at something new?"*
- *When and if they do evaluate something else, can we be involved?*

And, yes, with a company the size of the one you mentioned (name omitted here), I would have a stay-in-touch strategy where you make certain you stay in contact with them through e-mail, fax, letter, and newsletters. You want to be sure your name is at the forefront when and if they do decide to do something.

Gary's Results after Using the Questions

Art, I wanted to thank you for e-mailing me those sales questions you would ask in regard to large accounts. I was facing an important prospect—the largest safety products company in the world, with operations in 25 countries and sales in the billions—and I asked the buyer the questions that you had sent me. He took the time to give me very detailed replies and even invited me to their corporate offices to meet with him in person!

Smart Calling Action Step

What will you commit to *do* as a result of this chapter?

12

Using Smart Questions

Sales Rep: *"Boss, I can lead them to water, but I can't make them drink."* Manager: *"You don't want to* make *them do anything. Just help them realize they are thirsty."*

You now have a prospect on the phone whose interest has been piqued by your Smart opening statement. You have accomplished your opening statement objectives to:

- Put them in a positive, receptive state of mind.
- Move them to the questions.

Yikes! They're waiting. What now?

What you *do not* want to do is to begin talking about your product, service, yourself, or your company. That would be presenting. Do it here, and it will create objections. Yet, it is what many sales reps do that causes calls to fail.

Instead, we will ask questions that serve several purposes:

- To help *us* better understand the prospect's possible needs, problems, pains, and desires.
- To move *them further* into a state of mind where they better understand, see, and feel their needs, problems, pains, and desires.

- To provide us with the prospect's own words and terms they use to describe their needs and problems, which we will then later use in our recommendation.

Let's look at what to ask, what to avoid—and what to do when we get answers.

Use Your Possible Benefits to Create Questions

If you have a list of benefits that you are supposed to recite on calls, you may want to throw it away right now. Every time I see one of these goofy things, it reminds me of what I shared with you earlier in the section on your Possible Value Propositions: "*A benefit is only a benefit if the person hearing it perceives it to be a benefit . . . at that very instant.*"

Otherwise, a benefit is nothing more than something you *think* they should care about, and what you think is worthless without their concurrence.

But actually—don't throw that benefit list away. We will build on it and use it to compile a question list, which will determine if the benefit indeed is meaningful. Here is the process:

1. Describe a possible benefit.
2. Describe under what circumstances that would be viewed as a true benefit.
3. Draft a line of questioning that uncovers those circumstances.

Let's use an example.

1. **Describe a Possible Benefit.** A distributor has warehouses positioned throughout the country so customers are never more than one day away from delivery after ordering, without ever having to pay extra shipping fees. Plus, their warehouses stock more items than most other regional competitors, so there is rarely, if ever, a backorder situation—meaning customers don't have to carry inventory of slower-moving items.
2. **Describe under what circumstances that would be viewed as a true prospect benefit.** The ideal prospect for the distributor is a dealer that has experienced situations when it required rush orders and consequently paid extra for shipping. Other situations would be prospects (dealers) missing out on sales because they did not stock a particular

item that their customer could not wait for—and so went elsewhere. A skilled Smart Caller might have learned this information in advance by conducting some social engineering with the clerk at the front counter who deals with customers all day.

3. **Draft a line of questioning that uncovers those circumstances.** There are a couple of different directions in which the Smart Caller could travel with the questioning. He would start with a broad, general question to prompt the prospect to discuss the ordering process and inventory. For example,

> *Smart Caller:* "Tell me about your plumbing department and what lines you are stocking."j

Then, he'd ask a few more questions about who the dealer buys from, his regular ordering patterns, and how much inventory the dealer stocks. Again, knowing this information in advance helps; it is easier to prepare the questions when you know the answers. I know this will not always be possible, but you can see how beneficial it is when you do get that information first.

In any event, he'd then pose an assumptive problem question: one that assumes the prospect experiences the problem and asks him or her to talk about it. For example:

> *"I see. What do you do in situations where a customer needs an item the next day that you don't have in stock?"*
>
> *"Tell me about the times you had to pay extra for rush delivery to get a part the next day for a customer."*

There are several strategies and techniques at work in this process. We'll explore those to make sure your questions elicit the best information.

Not All Questions Are Good Ones: How to Use Assumptive Problem Questions

Not all questions are good questions; some actually lead us to a dead end. Try to avoid asking questions like these of prospects and customers:

> *"Are you satisfied with what you're using?"*
>
> *"Do you have any training needs?"*

"Are you having any problems?"

"Is there anything I could do for you?"

These questions force the listener to do too much thinking. They assume that the prospect was just sitting there pondering a problem, when your call just happened to arrive at that moment so they can vent their frustration! Fat chance. Besides, the words *problems, needs,* and *satisfied* are vague. If their problem was major—or if they were unsatisfied to the point of discomfort—they would have acted on it by now.

This is not to say that they may *not* be dissatisfied or have a problem; they very likely could. They just aren't aware of it at the second you ask them, or they don't perceive it as being an immediate concern. Your job is to help them realize it—you don't tell them, though.

Instead, you ask assumptive problem questions. These are questions that assume rather than outright *ask* whether your prospect has a problem and gets them to think about it, visualize it, and describe it. Let's say, for example, that you know your competitor has slower delivery times than you, and that you carry time-sensitive products. Assume they have the problem, and instead of asking your prospect if they have any delivery issues, paint a picture of the results of poor delivery: *"What happens when you have had to stop the production line waiting for a parts delivery?"*

Now the same person who says they don't have a problem is flashing back to the day she caught heat from her boss for paying people to stand around—all because of one replacement part that didn't arrive.

How to Create Assumptive Problem Questions

Here's a simple way to structure these questions: Make a list of all the situations regarding loss or pain that could result by not using your product. Then, frame questions that very explicitly paint an emotional portrait of those feelings. For example:

Not: *"Do you ever have a need for temporary help?"*

Try: *"How often do you find your department with more work than you have time to complete it in, and trouble staring at you if you don't meet the deadline?"*

Not: *"Are you happy with your advertising?"*

Try: *"When have you spent money on any promotions where the results didn't bring the phone calls you expected?"*

You can begin these questions with

"What happens when . . . ?"

"How do you handle it when . . . ?"

"What do you do when . . . ?"

"Tell me about situations where . . . ?"

"What are the implications of . . . ?"

"How does it affect_____ when . . . ?"

Josh Margolis, a Smart Caller, shared that he has success with questions that begin with,

> *"Is it a challenge to . . . ?"*
>
> *"Are you frustrated because . . . ?"*
>
> And his favorite, *"Are you embarrassed because . . . ?"*

The Loaded Benefit Question

Similarly, this is a question that implies a benefit of your product or service by stating a problem you've solved for someone else. It then asks prospects about their experience regarding the situation or predicament. For example:

> *"Most of our customers found that they were having issues getting their deliveries within five days with the other service. What is your experience?"*
>
> *"Before they began using our service, many of our customers felt that their re-do rate was unacceptable because of all the wasted material. What kind of rates are you running into?"*
>
> *"Many people find it a nuisance to manually fill out those forms every day when the information is already in the computer. What have your people said in the past about reentering the data?"*

This type of question paints the picture of inconvenience in listeners' minds, and they are better equipped to visualize and feel it. If and when they agree, you have the opportunity to tell them how you can come to the rescue. The real power here lies in using a third-party example; it's much better than blatantly telling prospects that they have probably experienced the problem you can solve.

Smart Calling Exercise

1. Go through the three-step process, using your possible benefits to create a line of questioning.
2. Define the problems and pains you are fairly sure exist in your prospects' world. Then write out assumptive problem and loaded benefit questions.

Practice the Iceberg Theory of Questioning with the Next Questions to Get Better Information

Several years ago, I coined the term the *iceberg theory of questioning* to illustrate what we need to do on calls to get the best information. When you see an iceberg glistening in the water, what do you really see? You see just the tip, only a small portion of the iceberg. The bulk of it is below the water level.

The same is true when you ask a question: The first answer you hear is the tip of the iceberg. Everything below the water level is the good stuff, the information you really can use, the *reason* behind the initial answer. People do not buy because of the first answer they give; they buy because of the reasons behind it. The problem is that many salespeople ask the first questions and quit after they have the tip information without bothering to ask the *next* question, the one that provides the information below the water level, which will tell them why, precisely, the prospects or customers say what they do. And *that's* the information we need to help them buy.

The *next* question is the one that many fail to ask but that has the greatest payoff. Remember the old detective TV show *Columbo*? He always asked, *"One more question."* Let's look at a sales rep who does not ask the *next* question.

Sales Rep: "What criteria will you use in awarding the proposal?"

Prospect: "We're going to heavily weight the on-time delivery projections."

Sales Rep: "Oh, let me tell you about our performance in that area."

Instead, let's look at the *next* question that lowers the water level on the iceberg:

Sales Rep: "Please tell me why that's the most important factor, and what you're looking for."

In the first scenario, the rep jumped in and presented prematurely, talking about what *he* wanted to discuss. And after the *next* question, he would probably ask a few more *next* questions to dig deeper, magnify the pain in the prospect's mind, and gather better information. This would, in turn, help him make a laserlike presentation that would stir more emotions—and have a better chance at getting the sale.

Here's another example: A sales rep for a human resources personality assessment testing service finds out through some social engineering that the company he's calling on wants to implement employee personality testing for new hires. In his questioning, he asks, *"Why are you looking to do employee testing?"*

The prospect responds, *"We feel that we need to do a better job of screening our applicants so that we don't make hiring mistakes."*

The sales rep—who has been selling this service for several years and feels he has been there and done that—thinks he has a grasp on the situation and begins a presentation on the testing service.

The prospect responds by saying, *"Okay, that sounds interesting. Send me out whatever information you have, and we'll give it some consideration."*

The sales rep complies. He schedules a follow-up for seven days later. He keeps getting voice mail on repeated attempts, with no return calls from the prospect. The cycle continues. And oh, by the way, this experienced sales rep has a problem with lots of prospects in his pipeline and complains about prospects not buying and how he can't reach them.

Let's look at another sales rep who knows how to lower the water level and learn more of the reasons behind what people say.

Prospect: *"We feel that we need to do a better job of screening our applicants so we that don't make hiring mistakes."*

Sales Rep: *"Tell me more."*

Prospect: *"Well, we've hired a few people over the past year that just didn't work out. They seemed good in the initial interviews, but apparently we were missing something."*

Sales Rep: *"What do you mean?"*

Prospect: *"They were able to talk a good game, but when it came time to actually do the work, they lacked what it took."*

Sales Rep: *"That's not uncommon. What does it take to do well at your organization?"*

Prospect: *"We need people in our customer service positions who can handle repetitive tasks all day long without becoming bored, remain calm under pressure from irate callers, and be able to think quickly on their feet to resolve problems that involve some math calculations."*

Sales Rep:*"I believe we can help you with that. Tell me a bit more about your past experiences. About how many people have you hired that didn't work out?"*

Prospect:*"Almost embarrassed to say . . . probably 10 out of 20."*

Sales Rep:*"Wow. Any idea of what it costs to hire and train someone for that position?"*

Prospect:*"I hate to even think about it. After newspaper advertising, our interviewing, two weeks of product training and their wages, it's got to be a few thousand dollars per person."*

As you saw, the sales rep pretty much got out of the prospect's way as he replied to the prospect's statements with the *next* question each time, continuing to lower the water level on the iceberg.

Keep your prospects talking about their needs, desires, and concerns; you want the real reasons behind their initial answers to surface. The first important step in achieving this is discipline. Resist the tendency to jump in and present; instead, use instructional statements such as:

"Tell me more."

"Please go on."

"Elaborate on that for me, please."

"I'd like to know more about that."

"Please continue."

And when they touch on a need, embellish it, quantify it, and have them discuss its implications (particularly the financial ones).

Smart Calling Tip

One of the greatest questions of all time—one that can give you more information than you ever thought possible—is just two letters: "Oh?"

More on Quantifying Needs, Pains, Problems, and Desires

A goal of your *next* questions should be to attach numbers to pains, problems, needs, and desires. Whenever you can, prompt them to provide you with details for situations like:

- How much money they are losing because of their problem.
- How much extra time it takes to perform a task and the related pain that causes.
- How much more it costs them to get products delivered from another supplier.
- How much larger their sales numbers could be with a better solution.

It is much easier for you to show a potential return on investment, build value, and preempt any looming price objection when you have information like this.

(In their book *The Dollarization Discipline: How Smart Companies Create Customer Value . . . and Profit from It*, authors Jeffrey J. Fox and Richard C. Gregory go into great detail on this topic. If you are serious about sales, I highly recommend this book.)

Smart Calling Exercise

Identify the areas in which you can quantify value for your prospects and create questions designed to prompt them to attach numbers and dollars to their situations.

Avoid Questions That Scream "I Just Picked Up an Old Sales Book"

There are some questions that have been around forever and really have been worn out to the point where they sound cheesy. For example: *"If you could wave a magic wand, what would you want?"*

Uh, I dunno. How about you off the phone?

Here's a better alternative that accomplishes the same information objective: *"What would you like to get that you might not have now?"*

Another tired question: *"What keeps you up at night?"* While the premise here is solid—identifying their major pain—the technique is, well, a technique.

Better alternative: *"What's the top concern you're facing right now as it relates to____?"*

Smart Calling Tip

Want to sound smooth on your calls? Take a cue from Supreme Court Chief Justice John Roberts, who appeared at his confirmation hearings with *no* notes and nailed the answer to every question—because he had prepared for virtually *everything* that could be thrown at him. You can't script out your entire call, but you can anticipate answers to your questions in advance, particularly the ones you'd prefer not to hear. You should use these to prepare your next responses and continue the process as if you were role-playing the situation live. Studying what you prepare puts you in a much better position to handle these situations when they occur. That is the key to sounding smooth.

Questions to Learn about the Decision-Making Hierarchy and Process

It should go without saying that you do not want to ask: *"So, are you the decision maker there?"* But what *do* you say to learn who ultimately makes the decision to buy what you sell? I like questions like these:

> *"Who aside from yourself would be involved in this discussion?"*
> *"Who will you consult with as you plan this project?"*
> *"Who else should we include in our next meeting?"*

Asking about the decision-making process depersonalizes it, which can make it less threatening to answer for the prospect:

> *"What route will this decision have to take in the organization to finally get approved?"*
> *"What is the process on your end for moving this forward?"*
> *"What needs to happen on your end to get this done?"*

Determine What Annoys Them

Who *isn't* overworked and underpaid? Certainly not your prospects and customers, and they're always interested in ways they can ease their workload, especially clearing their docket of those time-gobbling mundane tasks. Find out what sticks in their craw and annoys them. Ask questions like:

> "Regarding_____, what causes you or your staff unnecessary work?"
>
> "What things force you to engage in annoying activities that you shouldn't have to do?"

Smart Calling Tip

Do not say, "Can I ask you a question?" That already *is* a question. So just ask the question.

A Questioning Mistake

A mistake I see reps make is asking questions like "Did you know that we offer_____?" or "Are you aware that we sell_____?" They use these questions during the fact-finding phase of the call and assume that these are actually good questions when, in fact, they are more like presentations. The problem occurs when you present before getting adequate information—because you run the risk of talking about details the listener doesn't care about. For example, asking, "Did you know we offer six different lines of printers?" could elicit a great big yawn and a "So what?" from the listener. A better question would be "What features do you require in printers?"

Smart Calling Success Story

A sales rep who called me had obviously done his homework and was a student of my material. I knew exactly what he was doing but found myself engaged in his message. He prefaced his excellent questions with hints of how he got his information. "While visiting your website I noticed . . ." "In one of your books you mention . . ." "I saw an article where you said . . ." "Your catalog has . . ." "In a past issue of your newsletter . . ." "Your mail piece has . . ." "I also noticed on your voice mail system . . ." "Your assistant told me . . ." "In one of your ads you . . ."

Clarify the Fuzzy Phrases

One of my many pet peeves is when someone says, *"We'll have to talk about that sometime," "At some point, we'll need to get together and discuss . . .,"* or *"Let's get together sometime and go over . . ."*

If it's something that needs to be done or discussed, and if I want to do it, I'll always say, *"Okay, let's do it now."* Otherwise—and you know this—it isn't going to happen. The fuzzy phrase strikes again.

When you hear a statement that is vague or wishy-washy, ask for clarification.

> Fuzzy Phrase: *"Let's stay in touch."*
>
> Response: *"Great idea. So you eventually plan to move forward with this? When?"*
>
> Fuzzy Phrase: *"We'll give it some consideration."*
>
> Response: *"Great! Which aspects will you weight most heavily?"*
>
> Fuzzy Phrase: *"I'll look it over, and we'll go from there."*
>
> Response: *"On what criteria will you base your decision?"*
>
> Fuzzy Phrase: *"I'll bounce the idea around."*
>
> Response: *"Good. Does that mean you personally are sold on it?"*

The Quality of Your Question Determines the Quality of Your Answer

Want better information? Review your call recordings, and analyze the questions you ask. Avoid using questions like:

> *"Does that happen a lot?"*
>
> *"Do you experience that often?"*
>
> *"Was there much of an impact?"*

Think about if a customer answered yes or no to those questions. You wouldn't really know any more than before you asked. Instead, get better information by asking for specific information: "How often has that happened in the past three months?" "What has been the impact on your department in terms of increased sales?"

Don't Ask What They Like Best about Their Present Supplier

An oft-suggested response when a prospect says, *"We're happy with our present supplier"* is *"What do you like best about them?"* I suggest *not* wording it that way, and my reasoning for this was formed while listening to a particular sales rep ask that question on a call. The prospect went into a long explanation of why his supplier was the greatest company ever formed, how he would never leave them, and how their service was excellent. He sounded like he was becoming a bit weepy in his adulation.

Since the intent of the question is to find out their ideal requirements and desires from a vendor, let's ask in different ways:

> *"What were the criteria you used when you chose your present supplier?"*
>
> *"What were the determining factors in selecting the company you're now using?"*
>
> *"When you evaluate vendors, what is the typical process you go through?"*
>
> *"If for some reason a regular vendor doesn't perform well, what do you do?"*

Ask About *Them*

For most people, their favorite subject is them. When you get them talking about themselves, their jobs, their personal experiences, fears, wants, needs, and desires, you not only acquire valuable sales information, you position yourself as an interesting person. All because you show interest in them as a person.

My friend and fellow sales trainer, Jim Meisenheimer, www .meisenheimer.com, wrote the book, *The 12 Best Questions to Ask Customers*. One of those questions asks about them, personally: "What are your responsibilities?" Ask that question, sit back, and listen to the valuable information they will provide you about how to sell to them.

Use Benefit Questions Instead of Inane Leading Ones

Many hard-sell salespeople and trainers suggest the use of leading questions to evoke a positive response, such as

> *"Of course you would like to save money on your supplies, wouldn't you?"*

"Naturally, if you could increase production, you would want that, wouldn't you?"

"Quality is important to you, isn't it?"

Don't use them. These questions are inane, and they put listeners on the spot. They're backed into a corner where they look and feel like an idiot unless they answer the way the questioner wants them to. You might as well just say, *"Of course you don't want to be stupid, do you?"*

However, the premise behind the inane questions—to prompt prospects to agree that they might be interested in what you have to offer—shouldn't be discarded. One way to accomplish this is to present a beneficial situation from another customer's perspective, and then ask prospects if that appeals to them. For example:

"Jane, many of our clients in the garment industry have been able to save 15 percent on their seasonal purchases by using our buying network. Is that something you'd like to learn more about?"

"Jason, we're established with many of the largest corporate headquarters here in town as a printer that can provide quick turnaround when their in-house shops can't. Would you ever have a need for a service like that?"

Using questions according to this formula is less threatening than the inane questions and opens up the conversation to deeper questioning and a further examination of their specific needs.

Economize Your Questions

Don't use two or three questions when one will do. For example,

"Is there a particular person who handles that function in your department?"
"Yes."
"Oh, who would that be?"
Better alternative: *"Who handles that function in your department?"*

Here's another:

"Do you ever experience variations in quality?"

"Yes."

"*What do you experience?*"

Better alternative: "*Please tell me what you experience regarding varia-tions in quality.*"

Smart Calling Action Steps

What else will you commit to *do* as a result of this chapter?

The More Important Side of the Question

Listening

I t's an amusing contradiction: Good salespeople are typically viewed as smooth talkers who can woo their audience with their words. Actually, the *best* salespeople are those who listen more than they talk and know when to shut up.

Everyone knows how to listen. We've done it all of our lives. Why, then, do so few people do it well? As a sales manager once told me: "My salespeople like to listen—to themselves talk."

In this brief chapter, I'll reemphasize the obvious: You need to *listen* to prospects in order to be most effective. I'll also share a few techniques to help you become even better at it.

Get More and Better Information by Simply *Letting* Them Talk

I approached the checkout counter at my local Walgreens. In my hands, I had a box of disposable latex gloves and a funnel. (I know. I realized the same thing when I got to the counter. Looked a bit weird.)

The clerk was an 18-year-oldish kid with multicolored semi-Mohawk hair, sporting numerous tattoos and lots of metal adorning his face. His head was down, tapping feverishly on his Smartphone with both thumbs. After I set my items down, he caught a glimpse of them. He tilted toward me a bit, so I could see one eye, with a pierced eyebrow slightly raised.

"*They're for cooking,*" I was compelled to blurt out.

His expression was frozen.

"*I'm catering the end-of-season banquet for the high school softball team. Eighty people.*"

He stared blankly.

"*I have a barbeque cooking team. Our competitions are done for the year, so we sometimes do something like this just to stay in practice.*"

His eyes were glassy, like fish in the ice counter at the market.

"*Oh, the gloves. Yeah, those. We use the gloves when preparing the meat and when we're serving. And the funnel, well, we make our own sauce, and we use the funnel to pour it into bottles.*"

His expression changed slightly to one that in any language says, "*Riiiiiiiiight. Whatever.*"

After getting my change and walking out the door, I realized that I just volunteered lots of information, and this kid said . . . almost nothing. He executed it to perfection. Not that he cared about the information, though. Reminds me of an old Jerry Seinfeld comedy routine where he asked in that Seinfeld tone, "*So why do people feel compelled to explain why they do what they do?*"

I even noticed it yesterday when a guy in front of me at the convenience store said to the clerk, "*I'd like change for a dollar, please.*" (pause) "*It's for the newspaper machine outside.*"

Your prospects and customers will also continue talking—if you let them. Practice this. Force yourself if you need to.

It's a simple rule: Speak less, sell more. If you allow them, people will go to great lengths to explain why they think, feel, and act the way they do. And that information will help you help them buy. Let's look at a simple technique to do that.

Your Most Powerful Listening Tool: The Pause

The right word may be effective, but no word was ever as effective as a rightly-timed pause.

—Mark Twain

Perhaps you already do it well. Most people don't. Right now, just be silent for two seconds.

There, you did it. That's all I'm asking.

Pause . . . more on your Smart Calls and in all of your conversations. Make an effort to pause at two points in the communications process on the phone and off:

1. Pause . . . after you ask a question.
2. Pause . . . after you hear an answer.

Not just a brief pause, but a two- to three-second pause. Here are some of the benefits of this technique:

He had occasional flashes of silence that made his conversation perfectly delightful.

—Sydney Smith

- You won't feel compelled to continue talking after asking the question if you force yourself to pause. People don't always immediately answer, and pausing gives them the opportunity to think a bit.
- The number and length of responses will increase. People feel more comfortable when you give them time to frame their answers, which will probably be more comprehensive.
- The amount of unsolicited information will increase. By not jumping in immediately after they've answered, they're given a little time to contemplate what they've just said, which may prompt additional comments.
- You'll have more time to understand what they've said. Since you know you're going to pause, you can spend all of your listening time focused on the message, not on what you will say next.
- You'll have more time to formulate your next question or statement—which will be more meaningful since you'll possess more relevant information.

Oh, I know this can be difficult for people who get edgy when there's silence on a call. Here's how to get over that and resist the urge to jump in or keep talking: Just picture the scenario when you're with people in person, keeping in mind what they're doing during the silent times—thinking, stroking their chin, eyes gazing upward, pondering your offer. They are doing the same on the phone. Practice this on the phone and in all areas of your life. You'll find you get more information than you ever have.

Listen for Their Key Terminology

On my own past four sales calls with prospects who contacted me looking for training, I listened very carefully and looked for their key words. I heard:

"Here's our challenge . . ."
"Our biggest problem is . . ."
"Where we need work is . . ."
"Where we're not up to par is . . ."

Of course, I took notes and wrote down exactly what they said, and after hearing each one, I simply replied with, *"Tell me more about that."* All of them continued, pouring out their pains and problems in response. It's a lot easier when people sell themselves. We often just need to get out of the way. (You should also use their exact terminology later when you make your recommendation, since they will not disagree with what they said.)

How to Make Eye Contact by Phone

I was recently having dinner at a nice Italian restaurant while on a speaking engagement in Chicago. My waiter was outstanding: very attentive, but not hovering. It seemed as though he always magically appeared at the right moment. However, one thing about him seemed a bit unusual: He didn't make eye contact when he spoke. Every time he talked, he would look down at his shoes. It definitely affected my overall perception of him and even made me a bit uncomfortable.

This got me thinking about eye contact by phone.

Of course, we can't see each other by phone, but we can feel the vibes—the same vibes created by eye contact or lack thereof. Let's look at some ways to make that verbal and vocal eye contact by phone.

Verbal Nods

When we talk to someone in person, we use facial expressions and body language (like nods of the head) in addition to eye contact to indicate that we're interested in the conversation. But what do you do by phone? Be sure that you're sprinkling in and mixing up your use of such words and phrases as:

> *"Uh-huh."*
>
> *"I see."*
>
> *"Interesting."*

Encouragement Statements

Similar to the verbal nods, these further encourage the speaker to continue talking:

> *"Go on."*
>
> *"Tell me more."*
>
> *"Expand on that if you would."*

Listen When They Lower Their Voice

Pssst—want to know a secret? Sure you do; everyone does. How about when someone whispers some information in your ear? You pay close attention. Likewise, be particularly aware of what prospects and customers say when they lower their voice or whisper so as to not be heard by others in their area. This is typically sensitive and important information.

What Is Your Listening to Talking Ratio?

In his book *How to Get People to Do Things*, Robert Conklin shares results from a six-month-long study of salespeople. He found that the lowest 10 percent of a sales force talked an average of 30 minutes per presentation. And how long do you think the top 10 percent talked? Twelve minutes.

It Would Be Tougher to Listen Your Way out of a Sale

A sales rep for a cooking magazine I subscribed to called and said, *"The reason I'm calling is that your subscription runs out this month, and I was calling to see if you wanted to keep that going . . . orrrrrrrr what you wanted to do . . ."* (nervous pause) *"orrrrrrr if you just wanted to let it run out?"*

> *Many attempts to communicate are nullified by saying too much.*
> —Robert Greenleaf

Even though I had not given any thought to my plans regarding the subscription, his hanging *orrr* s and invitation for a no finalized my decision. He made it so easy to agree, *"Yeah, just go ahead and let it run out."*

On the other hand, the law of inertia was in his favor if he had chosen to stop talking and avoided the *orrr* and invitation after making his positive suggestion.

There are several elementary points here that carry so much impact—and they're violated regularly.

- Don't talk yourself out of a sale.
- Shut up.
- Don't make negative recommendations.
- Make positive recommendations and then pause, regardless of how awkward the silence might feel.

Here's another example. After getting the question *"What is your best price?"* I heard a sales rep say, *"Well, it's $799."*

No reaction from the prospect.

". . . but we could probably give you a $150 new customer discount."

No reaction from the prospect.

"And I probably can get another $80 knocked off."

"Okay, that sounds good," said the prospect—who probably would have bought at full price had the rep simply stated the price and shut up.

Smart Calling Action Step

What else will you commit to *do* as a result of this chapter?

CHAPTER

14

Recommending the Next Step

If you've made it this far with your prospects—and things have progressed according to plan—you now have them thinking about their needs, pains, problems, or desires. This is precisely where we want them so that we can present—in the most favorable light—how we would be able to help them.

But how do you know when you have arrived at that magic moment when it is finally time to talk about what you would do for them and recommend the next steps?

I can't tell you exactly what that is—for you, at least. Every situation differs and depends on lots of variables—including what you sell, your objectives, and your prospect's mind-set when your call arrived. Sometimes we get lucky and contact them when they are actively looking for what we sell and it happens quickly. Other times, we might never reach that point—since there is not a fit. However, I can describe the ideal time generally; it's when you feel that you have sufficiently moved your prospects to the point where they will be receptive to hearing how you may be able to help.

In my own experience, I've faced both kinds of situations. There have been times when I've gone just a few short questions before recommending, while in other cases, an entire hour went by before I told the prospect what I could do for them.

Regardless of when that point arrives for you, there is a suggested process for delivering your recommendation effectively. I also have a number of other tips to help you make it more persuasive.

Pitching Is for Sports Only: Recommend Instead

First, let's talk about a term that is commonly associated with prospecting and sales: pitching.

I know a little bit about pitching. I've coached boys' baseball and competitive girls' softball, called thousands of pitches, and worked with pitchers at a variety of levels. My own daughter was one of the top softball pitchers in the region, and I caught well over 30,000 of her practice pitches over eight years. When I watch a baseball game, I'm one of the geeks who studies how the pitchers throw to hitters in different situations. And while it's been a few years since I hung up the glove from competitive ball in an over-30 senior baseball league, I pitched some there as well. In fact, I even pitched against former major-leaguers in a Kansas City Royals fantasy camp.

I also know about pitching in professional prospecting and sales. It has no place.

Pitching is for sports, not sales. Just hearing the word *pitch* in a sales context makes me cringe, because pitching describes what amateurs and hard-sell, cheesy, pushy salespeople do. Pitching is one-way communication; it's the seller *telling* his story.

Remember the telemarketers who read something to you, went on for two minutes without getting any feedback from you, and then told you they would charge your credit card? That was a pitch.

From like-minded sales types, I've heard pitches referred to as "puking out a presentation" or "spraying and praying." It gives me visions of a listener rolling her eyes in boredom, looking at her watch, perhaps getting ready to slit her wrists with a letter opener.

A pitch focuses on the salesperson, not the prospect or customer. And *they* are the only ones that matter. If you put it back on the sports field for a moment, a pitcher is trying to defeat the ones to whom he or she is pitching. He's attempting to get them out, trying to make them look bad.

So what's the big deal? Why the rant about the simple word *pitch*?

Because words follow thoughts, and actions follow both. If people refer to what they do as pitching, they are *talking*, not prospecting or Smart

Calling according to the process we are covering here. They are present-ing what they want to say, which rarely matches the listener's interest. And *that* is why objections occur. In fact, objections are *created* by pitches.

Instead, here's a much better word: *recommendation*. I use that in place of *presentation*, since a presentation can be viewed as similar to a pitch.

Ahhh, but what has to come *before* a recommendation? That's right: information. And to get information, we must question. After question-ing, *then* we make a recommendation. The recommendation should be on-target and meet needs, since the prospects *just* told us what they need, want, or are otherwise interested in.

And *that*, my friend, is professional, collaborative Smart Calling.

People usually know when they're subjected to a pitch, and they often perceive it negatively. When people are about to hear a recommendation, they don't feel they are being sold. That's because they're wrapped up in answering questions and telling the salesperson what they're interested in.

Keep the pitching where it belongs: exclusively on the sports field. For the Smart Calling process, we'll cover how to make an effective recommendation.

The Smart Call Recommendation Process

It's not until late in the program during my seminars and workshops that I cover the part of the call that is usually the main section of lots of train-ing: the presentation of benefits.

That's because the best salespeople present only what the listener cares about—information that's based on everything else in the call process to this point: preparation, information gathering, working with screeners, interest-creating openers, and questioning. The next phase is the sales recommendation. Here's the next step in the process—to make when you feel you know exactly what it will take to fill your prospects' needs, solve their problems, ease their pain, or give them something they desire.

1. **Transition from Your Questioning.** Let them know you're done questioning and spark interest—again—by having them listen to you:

   "Luke, based on what you told me about the existing insurance coverage on your business, and the added liability exposure you have, I believe I have something here that will cover you completely, at about the same premium you're paying now."

2. **Paraphrase Your Understanding.** Now you will simply rephrase the needs, concerns, desires, and values they just related to you in your questioning:

> *"Let's just review what we've discussed so far to make sure I understand it completely. Bottom line, you feel you've been neglected by your present agent, except when it came time to renew your policy. And you feel he's charging you an outrageous premium for the amount of coverage you now need since you're manufacturing toxic chemicals. Is that right?"*

3. **Recommend the Results of What You Can Deliver as Well as the Next Step.** *Only* talk about what they told you they're interested in—period.

> *"Luke, I assure you that with us you would have your own account rep and would get the attention you deserve. And you would like the coverage programs we have. First, we would (describe each benefit/result with proof of each claim) . . ."*

Make absolutely certain that you are presenting the results of your product or service, commonly known as benefits. Use phrases such as *"What that means to you"* and *"Which means."* These phrases ensure that you're covering topics that will cause them to take action. And since you are probably presenting several aspects of what you sell, get feedback after each one. This is commonly known as the trial close, where you get agreement on what you just said. For example:

> *"Would that work for you?"*
> *"Sound good so far?"*
> *"Is that something that would save you money?"*

4. **Get Commitment.** You're involved in a conversation at this point, either answering questions or listening to buying signals. We'll cover a lot more on the commitment phase of the call in its own chapter, but it really is a seamless transition from the recommendation. The commitment entails asking for the prospect's agreement on the next action—which could be a face-to-face meeting, an agreement that they will view your webinar or literature, the actual sale, or many other possibilities. For example:

"Pat, based on everything we've discussed, you'd show a savings from day one on the program. It would make sense for us to get together and explore a few more details, and I could show you more options with it. Would Friday morning work for you?"

Smart Calling Exercise

Take the statement you use to describe the benefits and results you deliver. Brainstorm for the sensory terms and descriptions that bring those results to life. Then find several concrete examples of how others have already experienced those results. Commit them to memory so that they're always a part of your presentations.

Use the Words of Others to Be More Persuasive

I probably have more books on sales, communication, self-motivation, and marketing than 99.9 percent of the population. I've got them on shelves, in boxes, and now, filling up my iPad. I admit, I'm a compulsive book and information buyer, and I always realize there is so much more to learn. Anytime I read or hear about a book that will help me or my clients and customers, I immediately go to Amazon.com. They have been able to sell me a lot more than I had originally intended to buy by employing that cool technique of suggesting other choices of books based on the one I look at or purchase. I always impulse-buy a few other titles because of this headline screaming at me: "Customers Who Bought This Item Also Bought . . ."

This is brilliant from a sales and psychological perspective for two reasons, reasons that you, too, can use to make more sales.

Social Proof

Dr. Robert Cialdini—author of *Influence: Science and Practice,* whom I've referenced several times in this book—discusses the principle of social proof. He says that "95 percent of people are imitators and only 5 percent initiators; so people are persuaded more by the actions of others than by any proof we can offer."

This essentially means that if someone else has done it or said it, it carries more credibility than if we say it. For example, if I'm told that there are others who also bought the book I'm buying when I'm looking on Amazon.com, they are probably like me and felt these other books are worthwhile, so I guess I should as well.

You use this concept when you want to make a claim about the value of your product or service by giving examples of others' experiences or, better yet, others' exact words, which carry tremendous weight.

The People Are Interested in Other People Principle

I don't have any psychological studies or scientific textbooks to prove this principle of persuasion, just my own observations and experience. You could also call it the *People Magazine* theory or the reality TV rule.

Bottom line: People become obsessed with the lives of others. Why, otherwise, is there a long-running TV show where the premise is watching a bunch of people live in a house together? Why are there TV shows and magazines devoted to what celebrities do and wear and where they go?

I'll tweak this a bit for our sales purposes and say that in business, we are interested in what those who are similar to us say and do.

So how do we use these two principles in sales? You can utilize these techniques during the recommendation phase of the call by simply saying something like:

> *"I was just talking to another defense attorney who has the same challenge that you're running into, and here's how we were able to help him."*
>
> *"We've worked with 12 similar accounting firms specializing in audit work, helping them cut down their duplication of paperwork and increase their billings, ranging from 10 percent to 40 percent."*
>
> *"Joe Klein at National Motors told me that he has used both of the other major suppliers of network doorjambs and that we are by far the easiest to work with, and give him the most value for the money."*

Smart Calling Tip

Use precise facts and figures. Saying you've worked with hundreds of companies isn't as believable as stating that you've installed this system in 274 locations.

Using the Principle of Consistency

I never met the late Tim Russert, but after spending many hours watching him on *Meet the Press* and other news and interview shows, I certainly felt as though I knew him well.

Part of Tim's popularity stemmed from the fact that lots of regular people identified with him. He grew up in a blue-collar, Catholic, hardworking family and neighborhood, holding down several jobs throughout high school and college and then competing for real-world jobs with the more privileged people. I experienced the exact same things.

From a professional perspective, I always marveled at how Russert could take something seemingly complex and bring it to an understandable level. He'd get guests to answer a tough question, then pause and spring a video on them, where they were shown maybe a few years prior, contradicting the answer they just had given. The senators or candidates would then squirm and have to defend why the things they claimed were not consistent.

But of course, he never did it in an adversarial way. You always just wondered why thesepeople said what they did.

The science of persuasion calls this phenomenon the principle of consistency. Dr. Robert Cialdini also says that most people desire to remain consistent to beliefs and commitments they have previously stated. You can use this as well on your Smart Calls.

We already worked on crafting and asking questions to prompt prospects and customers to tell you what they value, want, and need—all the things you provide, of course. For example, I might ask in my own case, "What is the main factor preventing your salespeople from selling at full price?"

If they answer, "A lack of confidence in asking for full price in a competitive environment because they do not know the right questions to ask to build value," I would then ask how much money they felt they were leaving on the table.

After establishing a figure to dollarize the problem or pain, I would employ the principle of consistency in the following ways.

In the Sales Recommendation

I preface my explanation of benefits with what they had said, therefore framing my comments with their own words and putting them in a more receptive frame of mind to hear and agree with my recommendation.

". . . and as you had mentioned earlier, you feel your reps need to be asking better questions to establish value, which in turn will give them more confidence to ask for and get full price. Here's exactly how we would do that."

After the recommendation, we want to move toward the ultimate commitment: the sale, appointment, or next step. Again, using their words makes them more likely to agree.

"Do you feel that would help your reps ask the right questions to build value? Would that help you to keep more of the profits you're leaving on the table?"

Smart Calling Tip

A sales rep with MTI Equipment, Tim Spreda, stresses the importance of listening carefully to the prospect's choice of words, as that indicates the terminology he or she relates to. Echoing these words back to them helps communicate on their level and make your words resonate. Spreda shared the story of how one prospect, a buyer for a manufacturing operation, repeated the terms "safety and ergonomics" in almost every sentence. Naturally, Tim focused the recommendation for his materials-handling equipment on those areas and used those words verbatim.

You Are Absolutely Going to Love This

While listening to some recorded calls, I noticed a pattern with a sales rep. She tended to preface many of her statements with negatives such as *"I have some bad news for you"* and *"Are you sitting down?"* before she gave the price of an item. *"You're not going to like this"* and *"I hope you're prepared for what I'm about to tell you"* were a few others.

And not surprisingly, she continually got negative responses and results.

When listeners hear comments like these, they brace themselves for negative news. Regardless of how you're feeling and what you're thinking prior to the comment, you are now prepared to hear something negative. People evaluate information based on the state of mind they're in at the moment they receive it. While this particular sales rep's approach provides a negative example of the principle of preconditioning, you can use it to your advantage.

First, be certain you're not currently in the habit of negatively pre-conditioning your listeners. This *is* a habit with many people. Listen to your calls from the perspective of the prospect or customer. Thoroughly analyze your language to determine if you use conditioning phrases that frost listeners. If you do, catch yourself before you use them again. Then, get in the habit of establishing an atmosphere in which your listeners will positively view your information. And it's not that difficult; in fact, you probably encounter it regularly when you see and hear an infomercial on television. How often have you heard something like:

> *"Now, for a product like this that takes the place of all the cleaners in your cabinet, you'd probably expect to pay $40 or more, but no . . ."*

You can do the same. For example:

"Here's the good news."

"Keeping in mind all of the ways this will save you money on your operational expenses, the price is low in comparison."

"And now I'd like to share with you what people say is the best part of the entire system."

"This is something you might even want to write down for future reference."

There's an old cliché that states, "It's not what you say, but how you say it." True, but let's add to that. It's also what you say *before* you say it!

Smart Calling Action Steps

What else will you commit to *do* as a result of this chapter?

CHAPTER 15

Getting Commitment for the Next Action

W hen I give customized training workshops for clients, we always discuss the areas where reps need to improve. When they tell me their reps need work on closing techniques, I begin worrying. That's typically indicative of a larger problem: not moving the call and the sales process to the point where the close is appropriate.

I suggest minimizing the use of, or eliminating, the word *close* and replacing it with *commitment*. Closing implies an end; instead, you want to open and build a relationship. To do that, you need constant movement on each of your calls toward an objective, especially your initial Smart Call. This movement happens when your prospects commit to doing something between now and the next call.

The Commitment Phase Validates What Has Happened So Far

A football team doesn't throw the long bomb every time it gets the ball at its own 20-yard line. A man doesn't ask a woman to marry him after one date. Neither tactic is a high percentage play. And—just like on sales calls—to achieve the objective, you need to move forward and enjoy the little successes along the way. The momentum builds and the ultimate commitment is much easier since you've traveled closer to the objective.

Therefore, the close shouldn't be the major part of the call; it's simply the validation of what's been covered so far. Most football teams would be able to easily score a touchdown if they have moved the ball to the one-inch line. And the commitment we receive should be relatively easy to get if we have done everything else right up to this point of the call. *How* you do it is not as important as simply *doing* it; in other words, just running the play.

Your Attitude Is More Important Than Your Technique

Scan the sales section in bookstores or libraries, and you'll find lots of nonsense on closing techniques. Many contain tired old phrases that cause people to bristle, like the guy from the Better Business Bureau the other day who, after his three-minute pitch about how I *"qualified for membership"* (by virtue of having a business, I guess), would like to drop by at *"3:30 on Wednesday, or 9:00 on Thursday. Which would be better for you?"* Neither, I told him, since that would imply that I saw some value in meeting with him, which he hadn't shown me yet. He threw the long bomb too early, before moving the relationship forward, and tried to rely on the old alternate choice technique.

And there's the famous scene in the movie *Glengarry Glen Ross*, where Alec Baldwin, playing the sales manager, gives the impassioned speech, imploring his reps to *"always be closing."* What nonsense!

Techniques are secondary to attitude. Sure, we'll cover a number of techniques that you can pick and choose from so that you have a few you are comfortable with. But it's much more important to work on your asking attitude. Get out of your comfort zone, ask more, and ask larger, and you'll advance more prospecting opportunities and ultimately sell more.

It's this simple: Have an asking attitude, and you'll do it. Be shy about asking, and you'll miss out, and maybe even lose your job. Don't let that happen.

Smart Calling Exercise

I issue this challenge at all of my training programs: For a period of one week, ask for things you normally would not have, in *all* aspects of your life. On your calls, certainly, but don't stop there. At restaurants, bars, stores, with the airlines—at every opportunity, simply ask. You will hear no, to be sure, but you also will hear yes; you will get some goodies you wouldn't have otherwise, and very importantly, you will see how effective it is to simply ask more.

Get Commitments on Every Call

There are several scenarios where you want commitments on your calls. These include setting up follow-up calls to move a sales process forward, receiving commitments to simply meet with you, getting a promise to buy, and having the prospect pledge to do something in the future if things change. Let's look at each.

Movement Commitments

Never agree to place a follow-up call until you've gotten the prospect to commit to doing something between now and the next contact. (We'll talk about this a bit more in the next chapter on wrapping up.) It can be as minor as agreeing to review your catalog and selecting items they would like to discuss on the next call, an agreement that they will go through your web demo, a promise to collect their sales figures—the possibilities are limitless. Here are possible questions you can ask to get movement:

> *"What will happen between now and our next contact?"*
>
> *"So you will have those inventory figures prepared by the next time we speak, is that right?"*
>
> *"You're going to survey your staff and get their input on what features they'd like to see, and you'll have the information by our next call, correct?"*
>
> *"By when will you have had a chance to go through the material so we can speak again?"*
>
> *"What specifically needs to happen on your end to move forward?"*

"What will we need to do in order to make this happen?"

"When you are evaluating a product, what criteria will you use to judge it, and what will you need to see to move forward?"

Some squeamish types might argue that some of these questions are pushy, but they are common business questions that are logical to ask if someone has come this far with you in a sales conversation.

Smart Calling Tip

Here's a series of questions I have made lots of money with. Anytime your prospects say they need to speak with someone else, ask, *"Are you personally sold on this?"* Variations include *"If you were to make the decision yourself, are we the ones you would choose?"* and *"Is this what you want to do?"* If they say yes, then you can continue with the next commitment question: *"Are you going to recommend that you go with it?"* Or *"Will you recommend our proposal at the committee meeting?"* If other people are doing the selling for you, you need to be sure they are sold first.

Commitments to Meet with You

For some Smart Callers, the primary objective is to meet with the buyer. (As a reminder, I suggest taking the call as far as possible by phone to ensure you have an interested, qualified, hot prospect upon your arrival.) As with most of these commitment questions, the meeting request does not need to sound salesy or like a technique:

"Sounds like it would make sense for us to get together and discuss this further. Would you be available next Wednesday?"

"I have several options that I would like to show you in person. Let's set up a time to get together."

"Since there are going to be a few others involved in your process, I would like to sit down with the committee and go through the proposal. Could we do that next week?"

The Ultimate Commitment: Buying from You

Some of you may have a one-call close scenario that would allow you to go for the sale on an initial call. Even if you don't, the following suggestions will help you when that time does arrive on subsequent calls or visits.

When you do pull the trigger and ask for the business, make certain you truly are *asking*, not just wishing. I'll share an example with you. I was at a local Scottsdale big-box electronics store looking to buy a new computer CPU; I had gotten tired of lugging my laptop around all of the time. I drove to the store with the intention of buying—quickly. Not shopping, buying.

I should have been a sales rep's dream. The person staffing the computer department greeted me and asked what I was looking for. I told him that I needed something to handle document creation, web stuff, and audio production. I stressed the words "looking to buy" several times. He pointed out several models, explained the options, and prices.

And he waited.

I emitted all kinds of buying signals, the kind that make most of us drool. He responded with things like *"Well, we have this available"* and *"Keep this in mind."*

I did everything but say, *"How do I give you my money?"* wanting to see how long I could go before he would finally ask if I wanted to buy the machine.

Realizing that I could have wasted the entire day there—and knowing I had numerous projects awaiting me back at my home office and an 85-degree sunny day that needed a few golf balls pounded into its atmosphere that afternoon—I finally asked him, *"Do you want me to buy this?"*

A bit shocked, he said, *"Uh, yeah, sure."*

And I did. He got the sale. Most reps wouldn't have, in similar situations. There's a difference between letting someone know what you have available and *asking* them to make a decision. *Asking* gets action; merely telling them about what's available *wishes* for the sale.

For example, put yourself in the position of a prospect hearing this: *"And I just want to let you know that we do have these in several different models and they are in stock."*

That's weak compared to:

"And based on what you told me about your situation, the K-100 Model would be ideal to help you cut down your processing time. I have one in stock and could ship it today. May I do that for you?"

Naturally, the second one asks for a decision. Don't just throw your desires out there and hope they'll react. Be specific and *ask* (or *invite*) them to make that decision now. Sure, you'll get more no's, but what will you have lost? Nothing.

Will you get more sales? It's guaranteed. Just ask the people who get the high numbers now.

And, similarly, lots of people have been very close to getting the decision they were looking for—but quit too early.

I often do an exercise in my seminars where I ask participants to give me one method they use to *ask* for the sale or commitment. Usually I will have one or two who say something like *"So I'll go ahead and fax over the contract, okay?"*

Now, do you think that is *asking* for the sale?

No! What did the prospect say they would *do* with the contract? Nothing. And that is precisely what often happens.

The other part of that—the important part—is: *"And when will you sign it and send it back with the deposit?"*

Let's look at some others:

"Can we finalize the paperwork?"

"Shall we get started?"

"If you like what you see in the sample, will you provide a purchase order?"

"Would you like to buy it?"

"Why don't I ship you one?"

"May I sign you up?"

"If the proposal contains all of these items, will you approve it and go with our plan?"

"What credit card do you want to put this on?"

Smart Calling Exercise

Write down at least two specific ways you ask for the sale. Analyze them to be certain you leave no doubt that you are asking for the decision to buy. Practice reciting them so they will be smooth.

Commitment for the Future

You've done all of the heavy lifting up to this point. If you determine there is not a fit or any other shorter-term potential today, you could increase your chances for doing business in the future with a commitment question. But *not*: "Keep us in mind, okay?" Everyone smiles and says, "Oh, I will," in response to that. But we know they don't. Instead, ask a more definitive question:

"If you do decide to change vendors before my next call, will you call me?"

"The next time you need supplies, would you buy them from me?"

"When you send out your request for proposals, may I be included?"

Here are some other commitment ideas and tips to move the sales process more quickly.

Get Commitment with Nonthreatening Words

While people like to *own* things, they don't particularly enjoy *buying* certain items and services. So quit using the words *buy*, *sell*, and *sold* when talking with your customer. Instead of *"Is this the machine you'd like to buy?"* try *"Is this the machine you'd like to own?"* It sounds better, and customers feel more comfortable.

Why Not Try This Question?

Use the *"Why not try . . . ?"* closing question. It's a nonthreatening way for them to make a decision. *"Pat, why not try the deluxe model?"* Psychologically, they're *trying*, not buying.

Help Them Realize They Have Nothing to Fear

A common saying is that the word *fear* stands for "False Evidence Appearing Real." If you have prospects who are sitting on the fence, reluctant to take the leap, they often don't have a logical reason for their inactivity, yet they are afraid to make a decision. And they probably can't explain why. So help them recognize their irrationality.

> *"What's the worst thing that could happen if you did this?"*
>
> *"Let's look at the worst case scenario if you moved forward."*
>
> *"Let's think in the future for a moment and assume that you did get this system. Can you think of any downside?"*
>
> *"What if you just went ahead and did it? Is there any real disadvantage you can think of?"*
>
> *"What would be the drawbacks if you purchased today?"*

Or try this one:

> *"Let's say you did nothing. Then where would you be?"*

Asking for More Gets More

I have repeatedly suggested you think big. I also suggest you *ask* big. Negotiators use a technique called the theory of contrast—that's just as applicable in sales—which states that you should ask for more than you expect to get or offer less than you expect to pay. It's called contrast since the price, amount, or ultimate solution arrived at appears small, contrasted to what was originally asked for.

Employing this kind of request establishes a psychological standard in the other person's mind. If such a standard already existed—say, a price the other person was thinking of paying—the much higher asking price immediately raises that level. For example, when I decided I wanted a nice, high-quality leather desk chair, I didn't know the going prices; my expectation was, oh, maybe $200 or $300. Wrong! My eyes were opened, and suddenly my spending ceiling had risen over the $1,000 mark.

Investment professionals do this all the time. They'll ask prospects if they have $50,000 to invest if the opportunity is right. This not only scares away the people who have no intention of investing; it often raises the amount that an interested investor might start with, maybe from $5,000 up to $10,000.

The theory of contrast also causes the other person to feel good about the transaction. It gives her a victory. All negotiating should be win-win, and this helps accomplish that objective. If, for example, you're authorized to drop prices to win business, you should always start with the full price, which is more than you sometimes expect to get. In the sales process, you could use the lower price as a concession in exchange for getting a larger order.

Smart Calling Exercise

Think of all the situations you create where you ask. Examine at what level or amount you typically ask for. Now multiply that by 30 percent. Why can't *that* be your new norm? It could. Usually, the only thing that's limiting you is yourself.

Ask for Action, Not Permission

An article that originally appeared in the *New York Times* on October 15, 1997, titled "In War against No-Shows, Restaurants Get Tougher," by William Grimes, is especially relevant for us as salespeople. Here is an excerpt:

> *Gordon Sinclair, the owner of Gordon restaurant in Chicago, had an epiphany about 10 years ago when he began adding up the cost of no-shows and found that the grand total was $900,000 a year, a figure that got him thinking, fast.*
>
> *He made a change in the restaurant's procedure that underlines the curious moral status of a restaurant reservation, which is less than a contract but something more binding than "let's have lunch."*
>
> *He instructed his receptionists to stop saying, "Please call us if you change your plans," and start saying, "WILL you call us if you change your plans?"*
>
> *His no-show rate dropped from 30 percent to 10 percent.*

In other words, by asking a question and eliciting a response, Sinclair created a sense of obligation. Getting that soft commitment made a huge impact. *"May I send you some information?"* is asking prospects to give you permission; *"If I send you some information, will you look it over and we can talk again in a few weeks?"* is asking the prospect to commit to the next step. If you're able to engage them at all, you should be able to ask for some commitment—not permission.

If they're too busy right now—or their budget monies are coming in two weeks—*"Will we be able to talk more about this when I call back in a few weeks?"* is asking for commitment and implies that they need to be ready for that conversation when you do call back. Then, you have a reason to send them material, so they'll be ready. On the other hand, *"May I call you in a few weeks?"* is simply asking for permission.

People like to honor their commitments. If the call ends and they have only given you permission, why would they care what happens next? The ball is not in their court. But if the call ends and they've committed to doing something, odds are good they'll do it. And if asking for that commitment doesn't feel right, then it probably means you've got more work to do in building interest. Make it your goal on every call to ask a version of *"Will you?"* as opposed to *"May I?"*

Smart Calling Action Step

What will you commit to *do* as a result of this chapter?

chapter 16

Wrapping Up Calls and Setting Up the Next Action

You might determine on some of your Smart Calls that you are never going to contact that prospect again. You might decide that there isn't a fit, or they might determine that for you. Not a problem: Stuff happens, and then you move on. Hey, not everyone will be a prospect for you. Actually, a big part of being successful in prospecting and sales is realizing that quickly and not wasting time with people who have neither the potential nor the desire to buy from you.

On the brighter side, of course, you will accomplish your ultimate primary objective: getting a potential sale. Great, we're all good at handling those.

In many other instances, your Smart Call marks the beginning of a follow-up process, wherein your prospect will enter into a multicall sales cycle with you. Or perhaps while there isn't much short-term potential, there could be future opportunities, and you elect to stay in touch. In this chapter, we'll focus on how to determine who is worth following up with, how to maximize the effectiveness of those calls, and how to manage your time most efficiently in the process. Much of this occurs at the end of calls.

The Success of Your Follow-Up Call Is Determined on the Previous Call

Did you ever have a prospecting call that you felt went okay—you sent out literature afterwards and followed up—but then, on the ensuing follow-up call, the prospect suffered a case of amnesia, barely remembering who you were, let alone being interested in what you had to offer?

Or how about that gut-knotting feeling of staring at your prospect notes from a previous call as you prepare for the next one, racking your brain for—but not finding—what you'll say on this call that's more inspiring than *"Well, ahh, I'm just calling you back to see if you got my brochure"*?

If you've ever been in either of these scenarios—and most of us have—chances are that your previous call didn't end strongly, with a clear summarization of what had been discussed and of what was to happen next—both before and during the next call. Let's be sure this never happens again.

Here's an undeniable truth about follow-up calls: Their success is directly proportionate to how well you conducted and wrapped up your previous contact. Ending a call with *"Okay, I'll just send you out some literature and give you a call back in a couple of weeks"* virtually ensures your demise on the next contact. And rightfully so: There's nothing specific here; no connection between this call and the next; no synopsis of the problem, need, or interest (if there was any at all); and no confirmation of who's to do what next.

Granted, some of these prospects may have genuine interest in what you sell. But I find that many sales reps waste a lot of time chasing shadows—prospects who keep telling the rep to call back but who do not have one whit of an intention of ever buying. To avoid this futile exercise—to separate the buyers from the time-wasters and to ensure that you have a good reason to call back—you need to answer these three questions in very clear terms:

1. Why is a follow-up call necessary?
2. What do you need to do between now and the next call?
3. What will the prospect do between now and the next call?

Only if you are able to answer these will you have the maximum chance of success on the next call. You can't end a prospecting call by rushing off the phone as soon as possible by blurting out, *"Lemme send ya some information and I'll get back in touch"* and then expect them to be so exuberant over it that they immediately call you with an order. Normally, it results in the worrisome rep scratching his head before the follow-up call, fretting because he's coming up empty when thinking of something more brilliant to say on the next call than *"Well, what did you think of the literature?"*

Even if a potential client is interested, most people are not going to think about you any further until the next call—unless, that is, you give them a reason to take action. So let's go over how you can do this and how you can answer the three questions I mentioned earlier, paving the way for a solid follow-up call.

1. Why Call Back?

Too many reps commit to a callback but aren't sure why. A follow-up call to a prospect should occur only when you've thoroughly qualified the person you're speaking with as having the interest, the need, the authority, and the money to buy. Then you should know—in very specific terms—why this call is required. Exactly what action needs to be taken before the sale can be closed? For example, some types of industries, products, and call strategies stretch the sales process out over several contacts: The first call might be to qualify, generate interest, and send out a link to an online demo. The second call would be a fact-finding mission to gather enough information for a proposal, and so on. However, other salespeople operate on a one- or two-call close system. It is in these cases that sales reps should know why they are calling again if a sale isn't accomplished on the first or second contact. Perhaps upper-level management needs to sign off on such a purchase, or the prospect truly does need to talk it over with someone. Whatever the case, be sure you know exactly why that decision can't be made today. And be sure it is a real reason: it is the hobby of some prospects to keep salespeople twisting in the wind, teasing them with a decision that never may occur, providing excuses like "We're still evaluating it" and "It still is under discussion. (See our discussion on clarifying fuzzy phrases in the Questioning chapter.)

2. What Will You Do?

The second question you need to answer is: What do you need to do between now and the next call? This could involve sending out or checking on a price quote or researching for competitive information. The point is this: Let prospects know what you will be doing for them, and then do it.

3. Assign Homework

Finally, to get prospects involved, you need to assign homework. If they are truly interested (and they are, because you are calling them back—right?), then you need to get them to commit to doing something between now and the next call. For example, they'll talk it over with their boss or find out specifically when they will be meeting. Get their assurance that they are going to recommend your products in the meeting. This is critical, since if they won't agree to do something— anything—before the next contact, it's a sign that they really don't see enough value in taking action. A few ways to breach these topics are:

"Are you going to recommend to your boss that this is what you do?"

"What will happen on your end when you receive the sample?"

"What will happen between now and our next call?"

If, for instance, they promise to study your product materials, then point out particular areas they would be interested in—and then get their commitment that they are going to read it:

"Okay, John, to review: Before our next conversation, I'm going to e-mail the comparison report, which you will have on Friday. I'll highlight the page number you should study to get the figures you need. On Monday, you'll be meeting with your boss and presenting my proposal with your recommendation at that time, right? Good. What other information might I be able to provide that would help in the meeting?"

To help qualify and solidify a prospect's commitment, ask her to send *you* something after a call. For example, a brochure, product sample, or invoice from a present supplier. It gets her more involved and gives you useful information.

Summarizing the Call

The call ending is so critical to your follow-up success that we should break down its components even further. Here's what you should cover at the end of your calls to ensure a fluid transition from this contact to the next. (By the way, all of this presumes you didn't get a sale—since we're all pretty good at wrapping up those calls.)

The Need or Problem and Their Interest

Revisit what they are interested in and why.

What They Will Do

At the very minimum, you should get a commitment that they will read your material and prepare questions, test your sample and evaluate it according to criteria you've both discussed, and take your proposal to the committee with their recommendation. *This is critical!* If you don't get a commitment for action, this person might not ever become a customer. Asking for and getting some type of action commitment is my way of tightly qualifying people. Again, if they're not taking action, why are you calling back?

What You'll Do

Review what you'll do, what you'll send, who you'll speak with, or whatever you promised.

When You'll Talk Next

Don't say, "How 'bout I call you in a couple of weeks?" Let them give you a date and tie it to their commitment: *"Carol, by what date do you think you will have collected all of the inventory figures we'll need for our next conversation?"*

Not only do you have a date but also, again, you have their commitment that they'll perform their duties.

The Next-Call Agenda

Go over what's to happen next; it plants a seed as to what they should expect on the following call. Here's an example of how:

> *"Let me go through what we've covered today. You feel that Advantage Inc. will provide you with better availability, you like our customer service policies, and while you do want to get going with that new inventory program we offer, you need to wait to get funding in the next budget, which you're going to suggest. And we'll plan on talking on May 5, when I call you again."*

Smart Calling E-Mail Tip

Right after your call, send an e-mail to summarize the conversation and what is to happen between now and the next call. Then, send another with a similar message. You now will have had two more touches before your next contact, which will help to ensure that prospects did what they promised.

How to Set a Specific Time for the Follow-Up Call

To further cement the likelihood of success on the follow-up call, I suggest setting a specific time for your next call. What's interesting to me is that most telephone sales reps say this at the end of their call: *"Okay, Mary, I'll just plan on giving you a call back in a couple of weeks."*

What if you were going out to meet someone at their office and said something similar? *"So Mary, I'll just plan on popping in and giving my demonstration, maybe in a couple of weeks."*

When you suggest a specific time for a telephone appointment and treat it just as you would a face-to-face appointment, you send a clear message that your time is valuable (as is your contact's) and that what you're going to discuss is significant. Granted, you might not be able to logistically set an appointment for every call you place—nor would you want to—but everyone has those important follow-up contacts worthy of an appointment.

Most people view the phone as a less formal tool and aren't used to setting phone appointments. That's okay; it's actually something that you can use to your advantage. Requesting a phone appointment shows that both your time and theirs is valuable—and that you are therefore not a typical sales rep.

You need to be specific in setting your appointments. Meekly suggesting that you speak again "next Thursday afternoon" is vague and easy for the prospect to disregard. He or she is really thinking, *Sure, you can call then. I don't know if I'll be here or not, and it's really not that important anyway.*

So, you need to be firm and set a solid appointment. Here's how.

"Mike, let's schedule our next conversation. You mentioned you will have tested the sample by next Thursday, so does Friday look good for us to speak again?" Assuming the prospect affirms, continue with *"Good, do you have your calendar handy? Is there any time better than another? Morning, maybe?"*

Wait for his answer, check your schedule, and then narrow down the choice: *"Okay, please put me down for 11:15, your time, I'll e-mail an invite, and I'll call you. Does that work?"* Place emphasis on "your time" and "I'll call you" so you're clear on the responsibilities. End with: *"I've got you on my calendar, and unless I hear from you otherwise, I'll call you next Friday at 11:15. And if you have the sample and your notes ready then, we can go over them."*

Again, this reviews the details, reminds your prospect of what he or she is going to do before the call, and sets an agenda for the next contact.

Many of the people you speak with may be caught off guard by this approach. However, when they realize you are serious, they recognize that you are different from many of the other salespeople who call them, and they will remember you for your professionalism.

Smart Calling Tips

1. Ask your prospects if they receive meeting invitations by e-mail, and if so, send one to them. (Don't assume everyone uses the same technology as you.)
2. If their assistants keep their calendar, tell them that you will speak with that person to arrange the next call.

What to Put in Your Notes to Ensure a Great Follow-Up Call

Planning a great follow-up call requires that you take great notes from the previous call. So what should you record in your postcall? I use my ACTION sales model as a prompt for what I should cover during the call and what to put in the notes afterward so I can plan for the next. ACTION serves as an acronym for my to-do list; each letter of the word represents a category of information I need or something I'll do.

Authority. What is the specific decision-making hierarchy, including users, influencers, and money controllers? This is much more than just the name and title of the decision maker. It requires that I map the entire journey the decision-making process needs to take.

Commitment. What did your prospects commit to *do* as a result of the call?

Timing. When will they buy, and when will we speak next?

Interest/Need. What, specifically, are they interested in, and why?

Overview. Did I summarize at the end of the call what is to happen before our next contact?

Notes. All of this relevant information needs to be recorded in your notes. Create or update your information in each of these categories, Also include in your notes:

Information You Need on the Next Call. Remind yourself what to ask next time.

Possible Next-Call Objectives. What better time to partially plan your next contact than while this one is still fresh in your mind?

Opening Statement Ideas. Ditto the previous reason.

What's that, you say? Can't take the time after a call to do all of this? Think again. These steps actually save you time in preparing your next call and ensure that your calls are as solid as possible.

Use a Last-Resort Question before Giving Up

When an advertising sales rep called my office recently, I quickly and courteously notified her that I wasn't a good prospect and that we shouldn't waste our time speaking further. She said, *"Well, how about if I send you out a media kit anyway, and you can look at it and I'll give you a call back."*

I reiterated that I didn't need a kit, since I wasn't a potential buyer, and I was already very familiar with the publication.

She sent the kit. (Probably had a quota for getting X number of lit kits out, without regard for whether the person was interested.) Then she called a few days later and said, "I sent you the material and was wondering if you got it."

Trying to maintain my cool, I said, *"Look, I told you last time I wasn't a prospect for you, and you wasted your time, your printing, your postage, and my time with this call."*

In a situation like this, she should have used a last-resort technique on the initial call. After recognizing that I honestly wasn't a potential buyer, she could have said, *"Could you ever see situations changing where this would even be a possibility for you?"* If I had answered yes, it would have provided an opening for her to ask, *"What would those situations be?"* That would have given her the opportunity to at least stay on the call and ask me questions to determine if there were any need areas she could fill. It might have also been an opportunity for her to help me realize that maybe I did not have enough information about her product and that perhaps I was indeed a prospect for what she was selling.

Smart Calling Exercise

How to Get a Graduate Degree in Sales

One of the simplest ways to improve and become wildly successful in sales presents itself to you every day, multiple times. I bet you're not taking advantage of it. And doing so can earn you a graduate degree in sales.

Nothing magic, secret, or dramatic here: it simply entails taking a moment to briefly review every call you place. We don't learn nearly as much performing an activity as we do after it, by reviewing and analyzing our experiences. You can earn a graduate degree by simply assessing your calls and committing to take action where improvement is needed. It's a short, two-question process:

1. Ask, "What did I like about this call?"
   Reinforce a deed well done. What gets rewarded gets repeated.
2. Ask, "What would I have done differently?"
   Notice the wording here. It's positive and proactive and provides you something to work on and learn from. Don't ask the destructive question, "What didn't I like?" and don't darken your attitude with self-talk like, "I really blew that call." Instead, ponder what you could have done differently. This allows you to replay the call, conduct a mental role play, and search for phrases you'll use next time.

And that's how you improve and earn better than a graduate degree in the process.

Smart Calling Action Step

What will you commit to *do* as a result of this chapter?

SECTION
FOUR

Putting It All Together

How to *Sound* Smart

Effective Telephone Communication

I'm assuming that if and when you visit a prospect or customer, you are concerned with your appearance. You certainly wouldn't look like you just crawled out of bed, nixed the showering, shaving, grooming, and makeup, having thrown on tattered clothes and beat-up shoes.

However, that's the impression some people give over the phone. You can probably recall some of them right now. Just as you form impressions of others within seconds over the phone, they do the same with you. If your calling "look" resembles what I described earlier, it can negate everything you say, since how you say it will quickly alienate the prospect.

The good news is that it's easier and quicker to modify and improve the way you sound than it is the way you look. There's no dieting, sweating, vitamins, or surgery required, just some knowledge and practice. Let's explore how.

Don't Sound Like a Salesperson

Whenever I conduct customized training and presentations for companies and associations, I ask for recordings of phone calls as part of my preparation. On one recording, I heard a sales rep say in a very seductive, Kathleen Turner–like voice: *"Yeah, this new guy at my gym, he's totally hot. They might have to call security one of these days because he'll complain I'm staring at him. What I wouldn't love to do to that guy."*

She spoke with great emotion. Oh, she wasn't talking to a prospect or customer. She was talking to her friend, apparently elsewhere in the office. Seems as if she forgot she was being recorded. (If you're a client who has provided me with calls within the past two years and think this might be one of your reps, don't worry; I destroyed the recording. Well, the original, anyway.)

What was interesting about all of the actual *sales* calls I heard from her, though, was that she sounded somewhat like a telemarketer reading from a script—just going through the motions, with little feeling behind her words. But on the personal call, her voice could have melted headsets. Why the difference?

My guess is that in real life she sounds like she did on the call to her friend. When she got into sales call mode, her voice was the picture of her feelings about her job. Perhaps she looked at her position as though it were assembly line work, stamping out one call after another. Humans, prospects with real needs, were viewed as one more tick on the contact counter. She went through the motions like a robot, just mailing it in, call after call. But, oh, when she described the health club experience, I couldn't believe it was the same person.

Actually, it probably wasn't. And that's an all-too-frequent occurrence with sales reps. Far too many of them put on a game face that is much different from who they really are.

Here's a simple point that will serve you well in the way you look over the phone: Pretend you're talking to a good friend, on a subject you are truly passionate about. Picture that person as you speak with prospects. You'll sell more by *not* sounding like a salesperson.

Record Your Calls and Review Them Regularly

This is without a doubt one of the best activities you can engage in to improve and to make more money. Let's look at the benefits of recording and reviewing your calls.

You Improve the Way You Sound

You might have a great product or service with extraordinary value, and perhaps you have stellar sales skills. But you won't be effective if you sound like the AFLAC duck. Listening to yourself usually elicits dissatisfaction with some aspect of your voice, which is good if it translates into action. Perhaps you're too slow, too fast, monotone, too loud, too soft, nasal, or whiney, or maybe you possess one of many other common speaking problems. Your recordings can help to motivate you to sound like the person you want to be.

You Minimize and Eliminate, Uh, Filler Sounds

Because they can't see you, your prospects' pictures of you are painted by what they hear. Therefore, *uhs*, *ahs*, and *ums* are *amplified* over the phone. The first step in eliminating them is being aware of them. Your recordings are brutally honest.

Smart Calling Tip

At Toastmasters meetings, one person is assigned the task of "Ah Counter" and actually has to keep track of the number of times the speaker uses fillers such as *ah*, *umm*, and *er*. It is effective, since it raises your awareness of the habit. We can accomplish something similar on our calls. Pretend that someone is actually counting your *umms*. Try it! (Toastmasters, by the way, is a wonderful organization with local chapters devoted to helping members enhance their communication skills. I have been a member and highly recommend them: www.Toastmasters.org.)

You Realize Other Habits, Know What I Mean?

Think of that person who uses a word or annoying phrase, over and over and over, like, *you know what I mean?* It's like, annoying, ya know? Do you own any of these? The recordings tell you; your friends or customers probably won't. They're just thinking about them when you're using them.

You Hear Valuable Information You Missed the First Time

Although not sound-related, this is an added bonus for you. There's a lot going on in your mind during a call, and you might overlook some things when you're experiencing it live. Reviewing a recording of an important call can help you discover information you might have missed the first time. It's like seeing a movie a second time and noticing a whole slew of new things about it.

You Improve Your Sales Skills

Similar to the previous point, you'll pick up on buying signals you might have neglected, questions you should have asked, answers you should have given, and other areas you can improve on when you review your performance. Every successful performer in entertainment and sports reviews video of their performances. You should, too.

In addition to reviewing your own recordings, I suggest that you exchange them with a fellow sales rep. It's said that we don't know what we don't know—which means that we might not even realize that what we're doing is wrong or that there might be a better way. I know of reps who get together during lunch sessions weekly and take turns bringing their recordings for review.

Bonus Benefit of Recording Your Calls

Another benefit here is being able to use recordings as a review and preparation tool for calls. For example, let's say that you record an in-depth call with a prospect or customer. You proceed with whatever actions you agreed to after the call. Then, when it's time for the next contact, you retrieve the recording and review it as part of your precall planning. Their exact words are now fresh in your mind, and you might come up with new ideas for this next call as a result.

Legalities of Recording Calls

If you're wondering about the legalities of taping your calls, at the time I'm writing this, 12 states require that you let the other person know (which really ruins the mood at the beginning of a sales call). The remaining states require that only your end (that would be you) knows that the call is being recorded. Although I always thought I would be a good trial attorney, I'm certainly not one, nor am I qualified to give you a legal opinion. I suggest you do an online search using "is recording phone calls legal?" and you will find numerous sites listing the various state laws and, interestingly, different interpretations.

So how do you record a call?

Many companies have that capability built into their phone systems. If yours does, take advantage of it. If not, or if you want to do it on your own, there many options available if you search online. Obviously you will want to find something compatible with the type of phone, and phone service you use.

Here's one that I use that records digitally to your PC: www.headsets .com/headset/personal-usb-call-recorder/

Stand for Sales

The next time you're on the phone, try standing up as you speak. Researchers at the University of California found that we can process information 5 to 20 percent faster when we're standing than when we're sitting. According to Perry Buffington's *Cheap Psychological Tricks*, standing increases a person's heart rate by about 10 beats per minute, which in turn stimulates brain activity. So, when you have particularly important calls—or when you hit the wall after lunch—get on your feet to get the mental juices flowing.

And if you don't use a headset, get one. They are proven to make you more productive. I don't want to hear the arguments about how they don't feel good; just invest in a good one. There are a number of models that you can barely feel when wearing them. I personally use what I consider the best on the market, the OfficeRunner. Get it at www.Headsets.com.

Voice Improvement Self-Study

If you are really serious about improving the way you sound—both on the phone and in person—check out the book by top voice talent and coach Susan Berkley, *Speak to Influence: How to Unlock the Hidden Power of Your Voice,* www.GreatVoice.com

Smart Calling Action Step

What will you commit to *do* as a result of this chapter?

CHAPTER 18

Getting and Staying Motivated

Much of this book focuses on the mechanics of prospecting: what to do and how to do it. Really, though, none of that matters unless you possess the most important part: the mental ability. This is the desire to work and succeed, the self-motivation that drives you, confidence in yourself, and a positive attitude.

We could hand this book to people off the street to equip them with the processes and techniques for sales success. However, most would fail, since they probably could not handle the head part of the game. Conversely, I've seen some people who weren't necessarily blessed with the highest levels of intelligence and communication skills, yet were wildly successful salespeople. But they all shared one even more important characteristic: the desire to succeed, which translated into doing whatever it took to reach their goals.

The mental aspect of selling—and of life, for that matter—is a choice. You decide what type of results you will get each and every day based on your outlook on life, what you believe. According to my friend, motivation and achievement expert Dr. Alan Zimmerman (www.drzim merman.com):

> Beliefs are like filters. When you observe life through a particular filter, you can only receive certain information. The rest is unavailable. It's like having your TV tuned to NBC. You're not going to see any shows on CBS, no matter how hard you try. If you don't like how things are going, if you don't like how you're feeling, change the channel.

(By the way—one of the best books on motivation and attitude I have ever read is Alan's *Pivot: How One Turn in Attitude Can Lead to Success.*)

I must admit that I am a motivational information junkie. I've got shelves of books, tapes (yes, I still have those dinosaurs), CDs, and videos, and have been—and still go—to the seminars and rallies. And when I fall into a slump or a rut, the way we humans all do occasionally, I drag my butt to the bookstore and grab more motivational and inspirational books and dive into them. It's almost magical how filling your mind with this information can quickly pull you up.

What I find sad, however, are what I call the cynicals and skepticals— the people who make fun of motivational speakers. They also usually roll their eyes when there's an opportunity for any type of training or invest ment in themselves. They've seen it all before. And there's one more word used to describe most of them: *miserable.*

Just like their negativity toward self-improvement, that feeling bleeds into every area of their lives. They find fault with just about everything and everyone they view through their mud-colored glasses.

If you have more than a few people in your office, you probably work with one or more of these cynicals and skepticals. My advice: Avoid them. Their joy comes from making others depressed, and they'll try to pull you into their pity party—which can be fatal for your attitude and Smart Call ing achievement.

To be truly successful in your Smart Calling, you do need to possess the proper mental mind-set, and because of all the potential negativity you will encounter on the phone, you must be proactive about it. I can't motivate you. Your boss can't motivate you. Only *you* can motivate you. To help you do that, I'll share some useful information on motivation, attitude, and achievement. In more than 30 years of studying successful salespeople—and people in general—I have found definite patterns and behaviors. I'm confident you will find some ideas in this chapter that will positively affect your attitude—that is, if you want it to.

Never Get Rejected Again

We've already discussed how to never be rejected again in Chapter 5: to always have a secondary objective. Since fear of rejection is probably the largest issue hindering prospecting success, let's dive into it a bit deeper.

Those of us who have endured and prospered in the sales and prospecting game have undoubtedly taken our share of beatings. But we have always found a way to insulate ourselves from the endless barrage of no's and bounce back. As we've already discussed, you are rejected only if you *think* you are. Here are instances of how I've seen rejected reps handle everyday situations and taint them with self-defeating thoughts and actions, contrasted with what the successful reps—the achievers—do to constantly reach new heights and avoid what most people call rejection.

Rejected Rep: Burns through calls, hearing no after no, and slams the phone down after each—ending each call negatively.

Successful Rep: Accomplishes *something* on every call, even if it's not the primary objective. Even if she fails to make a sale or appointment, she always has a fallback position, something she can accomplish on every call, even if it's as minor as getting agreement to leave the door open for the future or just questioning the objection. A success, regardless how minor, means no rejection.

Rejected Rep: Lets the no answers pull his attitude down.

Successful Rep: Accepts the fact that he will get no's. Many of them, and then more. If this is a surprise to you, read no further and consider changing careers. Judge success based on your attempts, not just the yes answers.

Rejected Rep: Associates a no with who she is as a person.

Successful Rep: Doesn't take it personally. Realizes that it is not *her* they are rejecting, just the ideas she presented. Recognizes that the prospect or customer simply did not have an immediate perceived need at that very moment and that this could change in the future.

Rejected Rep: Mopes around after a no call or, worse, avoids the next call. I've seen reps who couldn't recall their best friend's phone number but could relive every no of the day.

Successful Rep: Realizes the last call she made has absolutely no bearing on the next one. The fact that she did not meet her primary objective on the previous call does not affect her attitude or presentation on the ensuing one. After she has dissected the previous call, she moves on and doesn't dwell on it. Instead, she wipes any negative thoughts from memory. She realizes her biggest sale ever could take place the next time she punches the keypad—and is always prepared.

Smart Calling Success Story

Here's a rule one of my clients has in their sales department: Sales-people cannot leave the office unless their last call was a positive one. They don't necessarily have to make a sale; it's fine if they meet an objective of qualifying a prospect and mailing literature, if that is their goal on the call (they have a several-call sales cycle). This ensures that everyone leaves the office on an upbeat note for the day and results in people eager to begin calling in the morning. Needless to say, sales are a natural result of this rule.

Overcoming the Fear of Calling

Have you ever scrolled through your contacts while planning your day, stopped at one particular lead or account, got that sinking thud in your heart, and then . . . bypassed it?

And did you continue doing the same thing for weeks, maybe months, maybe even longer?

If so, you're not alone. Many of us can trace this reluctance to fear: fear we'll get blown off the phone, that we'll sound like a jabbering fool to this intimidating prospect, that we won't know the answers to his questions—fear of *anything*, for that matter. And if we *do* manage to muster just enough courage to place the call while in this state of mind—isn't it interesting how often our fears become reality?

Lee Boyan and Rosalind Enright's book *High Performance Sales Training* explains a fascinating psychological phenomenon: The more we dwell on what we fear, the more difficult it is to forget it, and the longer it stays in our minds, embedding its visual manifestation and ultimately turning into negative behavior. (This quite often happens to some golfers when approaching a hole requiring a carry-shot over a lake.)

Austrian psychiatrist Dr. Victor Frankl suggests that to overcome fear, you must turn it into a ridiculous, absurd event in your mind and then allow the natural human reaction to absurdities turn it off completely. For example, when you hear of something that is totally off-the-wall, you shrug it off, saying, "No way."

Try this: Consider what is hindering your success, and exaggerate it to the extreme. For example, "I am scared silly of calling the Big Fish Company because my contact, Mr. Mackerel, is actually a demon with supernatural powers. He has, on occasion, actually transformed himself into digital signals and sent himself back through the phone lines, through the headsets of sales reps, jumped into their ears and attacked their brains, turning their minds into useless jelly, leaving their bodies slumped at their desks. In some cases, their managers couldn't tell anything was wrong for hours before they were discovered."

Absurdities like these are so ridiculous the human mind immediately rejects them. And once we can ridicule our fears, these problems lose their power over us. Harvard psychologist Gordon Allport wrote that any person who can figure out a way to laugh at his problems is well on his way to solving them.

So, what's anchoring your ability to excel? Create an absurdity through which to view it, and you'll see how truly ridiculous it was to begin with!

Say "So What?" to Your Fears

Call avoidance is often caused by fear of hearing no. A newsletter subscriber of mine e-mailed a very simple, yet effective way to deal with that. She said, *"Whenever I fear something, I go into 'so what? mode.' I just put 'so what?' in front of anything I fear. For example, 'So what if I get a no. Big deal.' It's a way of saying, what's the worst thing that can happen to me if I do it? It helps me realize that our fears are usually ridiculous and never realized anyway, yet they cause us to miss so much."*

Size Does Matter as It Relates to Your Thinking

Why do some people consistently produce at high levels, get bigger results, and make more money? Because that's what they expect of themselves, and this translates into bigger action.

The magnitude of your success is directly proportional to the size of your thinking. Big thinkers don't want to perform just well enough to meet quota; they anticipate blowing their numbers away and consistently earning more money and exceeding results like never before. It's quite simple, really. Think large, and actions and success follow, and the same is true with small thinking. The good news is that you're in control. As former British prime minister Disraeli said, "Life is too short to be little." Let's look at specific ways that big thinking translates into action and big results in your Smart Calling.

Calling Big Opportunities

Given the choice, would you call IBM or I.M. Little Enterprises Computer and Small Engine Repair? Big thinkers get stars in their eyes imagining the opportunities within a larger company: multiple contacts and departments, all potential buyers, the potential of huge orders and larger commissions. Small thinkers don't even consider approaching the *Fortune 1000*. They think, "Oh, they'll never want to buy from little ol' me." And with that attitude, they're right. Consequently, they are mired in follow-up calls to small prospects with little revenue potential, and they waste time catering to the demands of tiny accounts that probably shouldn't have been opened in the first place.

Action Item: Look at the top 10 to 20 percent of your company's customers. Analyze their defining characteristics, such as size and industry, and find similar prospects to go after.

Calling High within an Organization

Most sales reps have a level of comfort regarding the titles of prospects and customers with whom they speak. Some start low, and then they wonder why they feel like they're stuck in a molasses and Super Glue mixture when they're trying to move a sale forward. Maybe you've felt similar frustration. Starting low and staying there means you run into self-important middle managers who are overworked and underpaid and inundated with calls from other salespeople. Some are so afraid to make decisions that they make none at all, while the notes in your contact management system shows a series of entries like "Not ready yet, still in committee, CB in two weeks."

According to author David Peoples's book *Selling to the Top*, calling at a higher level is an easier and faster sell, less work, provides more value to your product or service, produces less competition, and allows you to charge a higher price. Anthony Parinello created a name for these higher level people: VITO, meaning Very Important Top Officer. In his book *Selling to VITO*, Parinello explains that VITOs are different from most buyers. Some lower-level contacts might worry about protecting their turf, impressing others, or holding on to their own shaky position. A VITO is straightforward and wants to improve the company's bottom line by raising revenue, lowering expenses, or improving efficiency. They won't waste your time if you don't waste theirs, and your potential rewards are huge.

Action Item: Call several levels above where most people start. A word of caution: Be thoroughly prepared to discuss how your product or service will favorably impact the big picture within the organization.

Setting Bigger Call Objectives

We've covered this in the section on objectives, but it's worth a revisit. What expectations do you have as you prepare your sales calls? Some sales reps approach each call "just to see if there might be any interest there." And maybe there is, so they quickly jump off the phone after saying, *"Well lemme send you out some information, and I'll call back again."*

High achievers, however, *expect* to take calls as far as they possibly can, so they do. They begin calls with a specific, ambitious objective, whether it's the sale itself or an appointment. A few points to consider: if anyone has ever made a sale at your company on a prospecting call, it therefore is possible. So why not make that your ultimate objective? Even if you don't reach it most of the time, you'll consistently achieve higher levels than you would have otherwise. And think about how much time you can save by moving others to a decision more quickly, regardless of what that decision ultimately is.

Action Item: Approach every call expecting to accomplish the best conceivable end result. You won't get there every call, but you know what? Your results over time will be much higher than with low—or no—expectations.

What's the difference between high- and low-performing sales reps? Self-confidence, belief in themselves, and expectations; in other words, the size of their thinking. But what about skill? While it's important, I've seen plenty of reps who had the tools to succeed without the desire or expectation. I've seen many more who would never be called naturals when first starting, but they expected to do well and found ways to make it happen. In his *Law of Success*, author Napoleon Hill said, "If you demand success of yourself and back up this demand with intelligent action, you are sure to win. There is a difference, though, between demanding success and merely wishing for it." Similarly, *The Psychology of Winning* author Dr. Denis Waitley maintains, "Every individual tends to receive what he or she expects. You may or may not get what's coming to you, but you will always get what you expect."

Losers typically anticipate little and get it. Worse, losers *expect* bad things to happen, and they do! You've seen these people before, the ones who can darken a room merely by entering it. They're the ones who consistently complain about everything from the softness of their chairs to the crumminess of their territory. All the while, the action-oriented expectant rep is doing what the other says can't be done.

How do you know what you *can't* do? I'm not talking about what you *think* you can't do; those are the self-imposed limitations you've believed up until now. When you analyze it, there's very little you're not capable of if you really try. So set a larger target for yourself and say, *"Why not?"* You realize what you've been missing, and you'll be more motivated as you go after your goal.

I challenge you right now, fellow Smart Caller, to burst out of your comfort zone in each of the areas we've discussed here. Think and act large—and your sales, compensation, and happiness will flourish in direct proportion to your thinking.

Your Assumptions Usually Come True

Nancy Zerg. You probably don't know the name, but she's the *Jeopardy!* contestant who beat Ken Jennings in 2004, thereby ending his unprecedented-at-the-time 74-game winning streak. She probably wasn't any better or smarter than him—she lost the very next game, leaving her own personal streak at one—but she managed to stay close during the main part of the game, then knew the last answer when Ken didn't. Game—and streak—over.

Nancy had something else going for her that certainly didn't hurt: confidence. In interviews after her victory, she said she knew that Jennings would have to lose to someone eventually, and it should just as well be her. In contrast, she spoke to other contestants who, before their games with Ken, were already resigned to the fact that they would lose. They said things like, *"Coming in second to Ken Jennings isn't bad."* And *sure enough, they came in second. Or third.*

> For myself, I am an optimist—it does not seem to be much use being anything else.
>
> —Winston Churchill

So what is your mind-set before your calls? Do you pick up the phone feeling that you're going to succeed? Or are you expecting the worst? We tend to look for, create, and get what we expect. Don't go into a call expecting resistance. If you must expect anything, expect success. And if you need to doubt anything, doubt your limitations.

Smart Calling Tip

When you're hot, keep at it. In other words, when sales and accomplished objectives are coming easily for you, don't stop to dwell on the success too long. Take advantage of the groove you're in and keep plugging away. Try to beat your best results ever. Success has an uncanny way of piling up when you are in a hot streak.

Will You Go for the Big Jump?

At the 2002 Winter Olympics, Eric Bergoust, an American, was the defending Olympic champion and the odds-on favorite in the freestyle aerial ski jumping. He seemed to have it clinched—except for the fact that Ales Valenta of the Czech Republic crashed the party by nailing an unheard-of quintuple-twisting, triple backflip on his last jump.

Ouch.

Bergoust was the final jumper. His jump would determine gold, silver, and bronze in the Olympic freestyle aerials, and it had to be as good as or better than Valenta's. In his mind, his options were win or lose. First or last. All or nothing.

Staring down the hill, Bergoust knew he had to go for it in order to win. He glided down the mountain, raising his left hand as he approached the ramp for takeoff. To the untrained eye, the jump looked good. But the excess speed made him fly too high and rotate too fast. When he stuck his arms out to his side to slow down the twists, he didn't slow as fast as he needed. He fell back upon landing. In an instant, snow sprayed like it was shooting from a snowblower in your driveway . . . and the defending Olympic champion finished 12th out of 12.

Dead last.

But Bergoust had no regrets. "I really had to risk it," he said. "I'm glad I didn't go out there and go conservative and finish fourth. I wanted to get the gold or last, and I got last. And sometimes when you risk it, it doesn't work."

Wow!

Just think of how many times salespeople have opportunities to speed down the hill, laugh at danger, and go for the triple-flip twist. Now think of how many times they take the safe, easy route by not making the tough call, not going after the big prospect, or not calling at a high enough level within a company.

Are you willing to take risks and go for the big jump? You will always be glad you did because the risks you regret the most are the ones you don't take.

Smart Calling Tip

Practice talking to people you don't know in lines, at the store, in airports, anywhere. Make a comment or ask a question. If you have any fear at all, it goes away quickly. And it's fun!

Sell More by Being a Kid

I'll finish up this section with perhaps the easiest way to be motivated and show success in your Smart Calling: Regress a few years, and be a kid again. All kids are born salespeople, but what happens when they grow up is that many lose the attitudes and behaviors that make kids great salespeople. Here's why we should be more like them.

No's Don't Bother (or Easily Deter) Them

When my kids were little (they're both in their 20s now), they'd react to my no responses as if they were hearing-impaired, ignoring the no part and relentlessly firing off their next batch of requests. They weren't *always* successful, but sometimes they were. They certainly got more than if they'd buckled to the initial no the way many adults do. And most kids aren't afraid to go to different levels within the decision-making hierarchy to get what they want. My kids especially knew where to go to ask for money. (They haven't grown out of that, actually.)

Kids Take Risks

I was mortified when, at eight years old, my son Eric roller-bladed up and off a plywood ramp!

"Oh, that's nothing, Dad," was the response when I asked if he was afraid of crashing. In retrospect, most grown-ups are too risk-averse, traveling the warm, safe, beaten path. What's the last risk *you* took?

If you're reluctant to live on the edge, consider one thing: Do you regret more of the risks in life that you took, or those that you *didn't* take? So why not throw caution to the wind once in a while?

Their Imaginations Run Wild

I remember when my daughter, Amy—about five at the time—handed me an abstract explosion-of-colors-on-paper. I smiled and sheepishly asked, "What exactly do you call this, sweetie?"

She replied matter-of-factly, "Well, of course, it's a city, Daddy."

Of course. Many of us fence in our imaginations by saying (and therefore believing), "I'm just not creative." Bull. Release your imagination, and let your ideas run wild. You'll be surprised at the results.

Kids Have High Ambitions

I know a six-year-old who's facing a tough career decision. He isn't sure whether he's going to play in the American League or the National League when he becomes a major league baseball player.

Ask any kids what they want to be when they grow up, and they'll probably tell you of their aspirations to be something great. Sadly, many lose this desire as they become adults and are content if they can cover this month's bills.

Do you have written goals that you are working toward? If not, begin today and determine what you want to pursue. And regardless of where you are right now, aim higher. You can get there.

They Have Great Attitudes

A trivia question on the radio the other day asked, "What do kids do about 400 times a day that adults do less than 20 on average?

The answer: laugh. (I've seen some adults who have really contributed to pulling that number down to about 20!) The moral: We should lighten up more. Who would you rather be around: the person wearing the scowl or the smile?

Kids Are Constantly Active

The word *walk* isn't in most kids' vocabularies; they dart wherever they go. Yet somehow they grow into adults whose sedentary lifestyle and attitudes contribute to a poor self-image and lack of ambition, not to mention health issues. You can spot the people in your organization with the poor attitudes; normally, they're the ones who shuffle from place to place. Put a spring in your step, move more quickly like a kid, get off your butt and exercise more, and you'll experience a better attitude.

They're Naturally Curious

As a trainer with more than 1,300 presentations under my belt, I've faced tough questions. But none ever exasperated me more than trying to explain the things my kids used to ask me when they were young, things

I always took for granted, like "Why is there frost on the grass when you wake up in the morning?"

In sales, we need to have that childlike curiosity because it helps us understand everything we should know before we make a presentation.

So, don't grow up. Think young. You'll have more fun and be more successful.

Smart Calling Action Step

What will you commit to *do* as a result of this chapter?

More Smart Calling Success Tips

To wrap up this book, I'll share some additional brief tips you can use in your Smart Calling.

Send an E-Mail to Find the Buyer

If you don't know the decision maker's (or makers') name and are having trouble getting cooperation from screeners or gatekeepers, then consider using electronic methods. Browse the company's site and look for the "Contact Us" information. Send an e-mail to the address indicated or to one of the departments that might be more appropriate. Say something like *"I was at your site and could not locate the address and name of your Director of Finance. Could you please reply with that information so I can contact them directly?"*

Find More Buyers Easily

Here's an idea for getting referrals: If you run across a start-up company while prospecting, ask your contact for someone to talk to at their previous employer. Often, start-ups are spawned from larger companies that are in similar businesses and buying like items.

Use a Calling Card

Here's a suggestion from Patrick Killam with Killam Publishing on getting to decision makers:

> I was reading a column in your newsletter about ways to get through to your party when they notice your number from caller ID and are avoiding your call. A great way that I work around this is that I buy a calling card (can be picked up at any local store). When you go through a calling card there are many different ways it can appear on someone's caller ID. It can say "Unknown Caller." It could be a number from out of state that goes through another phone network, etc. But, bottom line, I've had much success with this system. It's quick, easy, and you can do it from the convenience of your office at a minimal expense ($.03 a minute).

Draw a Decision-Making Organizational Chart

Knowing who else in an organization will influence the purchase helps you to formulate and implement your optimum sales approach. You can simply ask for this information: *"Tell me, is there anyone else who will be involved in the final purchase decision?"* When you find this out, it is helpful to create and update your own organizational chart of the prospect's company after each call. Fill in little tidbits of info about each person in his or her box. Then refer to the chart before each call so that you can put yourself in the prospect's environment, comprehend who else needs to be sold, and realize what needs to take place before you can win the deal.

How to Locate Other Decision Makers

We always need to discern the decision-making process within an organization and determine who the key players are. Here's a good way to learn that information without bluntly saying, *"So, what's your title?"* or *"Are you the decision maker?"* After your contact mentions someone's name— such as *"I'll discuss this with Jerry Smith"*—reply with *"So, Jerry Smith works for you?"*

They typically answer with something like *"Oh, no, he's the VP of Finance"* or *"Yes, he's the supervisor in charge of . . ."* In any event, they provide great info you can use to continue questioning.

Write Down Every Name You Hear

Every time your prospect or customer mentions a name of someone else in the organization, write it down. Ask about their title and function: *"You mentioned you're going to run it by Gary. Who is he?"* Gary might be a key player in the sales process. Find out for sure.

Follow Your Buyers

While listening to some recorded phone calls for a training session at Deluxe Business Systems, I heard a rep named Matt Davis reach a customer who said they were closing the company soon. After expressing his regrets, Matt said, *"Where are you going to go?"* Great question! That's a smart way of following a buyer and setting the stage to open an account with the customer's new company.

Be Ready When You Are on Hold

When a customer or prospect puts your call on hold, don't lean over to the person next to you and get in a conversation. You risk losing your train of thought and focus for this call. Plus, it detracts from the intimacy of the call if the customer comes back on line and hears you midsentence with someone else.

Get Referrals from within Their Company

If you have a customer within a company that has multiple locations—or many departments at one location—you probably haven't even scratched the surface of potential business. The hard part is over: getting the company as a customer. Now that you're in the door as part of the family, ferret out other opportunities. Ask your customer, *"Who else within your company also uses [does]_____? Who could also take advantage of something similar to what we're doing together?"* Prompt them a bit: *"How about other departments or locations?"* Even if they come up empty, you can ask them, *"If I can find other buyers on my own, would it be a problem if I mention your name as a reference?"*

Should Cell Phones Be Sell Phones?

The question of whether it's appropriate to prospect people on their mobile phone has provoked lots discussion, and I've even modified my stance slightly since the first edition of this book.

Personally, my rule is to only call a mobile phone if I have permission, or if it is the only number that the person uses (which likely would be a very small business).

Even though more and more people have gotten rid of their home phone lines and replaced them with their smartphones—and many keep their mobile with them at all times, even at the office—I don't feel it is appropriate to use that as a means to reach someone unless you have permission. Some way, somehow, still unbeknownst to me, an investment broker got access to my cell number, which I rarely give out. I didn't recognize the phone number that popped up but answered anyway and fully expected to hear a familiar voice. He acted as if he knew me, using cheesy "How ya doin' old buddy" words and tone. As soon as I realized it was a salesperson, my attitude turned to one of mild anger. I grilled him as to how he got my number. It went downhill from there, with him eventually hanging up on me.

Here are a few other related points:

- Even though some trainers teach this, I suggest not trying to get someone's cell phone number on your own when prospecting, unless it is offered by the assistant, or if you ask if they take calls on their mobile. Reps have proudly told me they've asked assistants and secretaries for decision makers' cell numbers by giving the impression that they know the person. Not wise. Just think of the reaction you'd get from the person when you call.

- If on the prospect's voice mail she mentions, "or you can call me on my cell phone," that implies permission. I'd still be careful, however, and use it as a last resort. If an assistant volunteers, "You can reach him on his cell phone," be absolutely certain that it's okay to call it. *"Is that the way she prefers to take her calls? You're sure that's okay?"*

As far as using a cell phone yourself for calls—I suggest a landline unless it is impossible. I always joke that you can do just about anything with a smartphone except actually talk on it. It amazes me with today's technology how poor quality is on mobile phones compared to landlines.

The same thing is true for Skype. The technology is cool, and you can't beat the price, but call me old-fashioned, if I'm having an important business conversation where I'm hoping to gain people's confidence and investment of many thousands of dollars with me, I'm not going to scrimp on my method of communication transmission. We are already handicapped in that we are missing 50 percent of our means of communication—the visual aspect—let's not handicap ourselves further by using a less-than-optimal means to convey our words.

Give Information on Your Voice Mail Greeting

I have to chuckle every time I hear a voice mail or home answering machine greeting that says, *"I'm unable to come to the phone right now"* or *"I can't answer the phone right now."* It reminds me of the TV commercial with the little old lady spread out on the floor, saying, *"I've fallen and can't get up."* Avoid *"I'm unable to come to the phone."* It says nothing. Give some information. Provide something more positive, such as *"I'm in meetings until 12 noon on Thursday and will return calls then. In the meantime, you can hit extension 25 and speak with Tom Smith."* Tell them where you are and when they can expect to hear from you.

Don't Create Interruptions

I was talking casually to a sales rep while touring a client facility. He complained, *"I just don't have enough time to get everything done. I have a hard time hitting my prospecting call numbers."* During our brief conversation (less than five minutes), his computer alarm chimed twice to announce new e-mail messages. He excused himself both times and whirled around in his chair to check the message. I asked, *"Do you do that all day long?"* His expression turned into a wince—one of those *"Yeah, I know"* looks we get when confronted with something we know we shouldn't be doing.

I know; it's difficult if you're in the e-mail habit. (Personally, I'm guilty. I even checked e-mail once as I wrote this brief tip!) But here are some ideas.

- Stay off-line completely. Check e-mail at set intervals, say, twice a day.
- If you can't do that, for gosh sakes, *do* turn off the alarm, the text, or the graphic pop-up that alerts you to new messages. This job is hard enough without inviting more interruptions.

Take Notes on What They Say *and* Mean

Sales rep Larry Feil shared a suggestion about taking notes while on calls. It's one thing to record what people say, but that's usually only part of the story. You should also note what they really *mean*. Larry suggests drawing a line down your paper, heading the left side with "What They Said" and the right with something like "How They Said It" or "What They Meant."

For example, in the left column you might write, "Says they will hold off for a month due to budget constraints." In the right column, you might say, "Sounds very tentative in speech. Very squeamish on this issue, even though he is sold on product. Sounds like there's something else here, but he's not comfortable discussing."

Smart Calling Action Step

What will you commit to *do* as a result of this chapter?

CHAPTER

20

A Smart Call Case Study and Makeovers

A "Healthy" Smart Calling Case Study

I take on a very limited number of personal coaching clients. There must be a good fit, meaning the sales pro has to demonstrate that he or she is motivated, willing to do whatever it takes to be successful, and is a student of the sales process. Chad Vanags met that profile and we decided to work together.

Chad is a sales pro in his late 20s who had success in the real estate business. He saw an opportunity with a young, progressive, rapidly growing company, HUMAN Healthy Vending (www.healthyvending.com). The company is a franchisor of vending machines that provide nutritious, good-tasting food options, and was on the Forbes' list of most promising companies for 2011.

Chad's job as a sales pro was to contact schools and sell them on replacing their existing machines with HUMAN's healthy alternative.

When Chad contacted me, he was frustrated because, like many quickly growing companies, they did not have a well-defined sales process and system in place. Chad is a process-oriented guy and decided to take matters into his own hands.

Chad followed the Smart Calling process diligently, spending hours on defining buying motivators, creating Possible Value Propositions and testing them, working on his research and social engineering, and developing interest-creating openings and voice mail messages. He painstakingly went through the questioning process, creating questions, anticipating possible answers and follow-up questions.

Together we listened to calls and refined each part of his approach. If there is a poster child for the Smart Calling process, so far it is Chad.

Chad rapidly started seeing the payoff from his work. In fact, he was almost doing *too* well. He was quickly reaching the allotment of machines he could place in franchisee territories. And within a few months he was given additional management and training responsibilities, including teaching his Smart Calling process to the other sales reps.

We'll take a look at just several parts of Chad's process, and some of the specific word-for-word tactics that he employed.

Chad's Process

Chad primarily targeted principals in public schools and administrators in districts. As it related to vending and nutrition, here are the motivators he defined.

- They are primarily concerned about revenue. Vending revenue has been severely reduced because of vending restrictions enforced by school districts and local, state, and federal governments. For example, one local public school district went from $380,000 annually to $30,000 annually. More restrictions are being enforced by the White House this year.

- Nutrition is also of importance to principals and administrators, but revenue is most important and measureable. Of course, vending is often the lowest item on their priority list because of the hundreds of other duties they have to deal with.

Chad would do a fair amount of research before calls, checking out the school district's site and that of the individual school, trying to uncover any relevant information about the district, school, principal, nutrition . . . or anything related to vending. He would also do social engineering, calling into the district office, determining how decisions were made, either at the district or individual school level, and calling into schools, asking about their existing vending machines, food service, and any wellness initiatives. In listening to his calls, Chad was quite proficient at probing and prompting people to share useful information.

His process then was to speak with a decision maker, generate interest on the first call, and then probe for needs, pains, problems, and motivators. Ideally he would take prospects to the point where they would share detailed information, and at the same time, be reminded of their problems or desires. Then he would briefly explain some benefits of HUMAN Healthy Vending, and recommend the next step, which would be an online presentation of the program. He would also ask trial closing questions during the first call so that if someone agreed to the presentation, they were about 70 percent sold already.

Smart Calling Opening Statement

Here is an opening that Chad developed for a specific prospect.

> *"Dr. Cook, this is Chad Vanags from HUMAN Healthy Vending. I've read your 'Turnaround Plan,' and Renee Swanson told me you're contemplating taking out all vending in Lawson Public Schools. Well, what I do is help schools get rid of the junk in their vending and replace it with healthier options, provide nutrition education, and can guarantee an increase in revenue instead of eliminating it. I'd like to ask some questions to see if I might be able to provide you with some information."*

If the prospect offered resistance with "We already have vending/ healthy vending," Chad's prepared response that we came up with was,

> *"Oh, that's fine, most schools I talk to do. We're actually quite a bit different and not concerned JUST about vending, that's why I wanted to ask you/them a few questions."*

With that response he wasn't trying to overcome an objection, just acknowledge the response, and differentiate himself in the process.

Questions

Next, he would move to the questioning.

> *"I know that vending probably isn't something at the top of your priority list, and I'm sure there are a lot of companies that call you just wanting to place vending machines in your school(s), is that right?"*

Our goal here was to empathize with the decision makers, acknowledge that they get calls all day long from typical salespeople, and get a "yes" response from them.

Next, we begin to frame the conversation and lead them a bit.

"Well we're quite a bit different because we're concerned about the same things you are and I'd like to tell you why, but first I'd like to confirm that my thinking is accurate. When it comes to vending I find that, normally, there are 3 main areas that (principals) are concerned about. One is revenue for the school(s); the second area is health, wellness, and education; and the last area is making it as easy and as hassle-free as possible. Would you say that's accurate?"

"Of those three, which is the most important to you?"

If they didn't pick any, then he would reply with,

"What, then, are the three areas you're most concerned about and which one is most important?"

In a coaching session, we had discussed the following, and Chad had it written as a reminder by his questions:

"NOTE: As you begin this next phase of questions, write down their answers diligently and word for word. You will be using their exact wording not only in the appointment closing phase but for the meeting presentation as well. This is CRUCIAL!"

Continuing on, if they answered that revenue was most important, he would continue to keep them talking about why this is important, what they're doing now, and ask about them things he learned from research and social engineering. Where he went from there was dictated by what they said. Listening was crucial. Some of his questions included,

"Why is that area the most important to you?"

"How important to your school is the annual revenue you generate from your current vending?"

"In what ways do you use the revenue to help your students grow?"

"How are sales and commission reports currently provided to you?"

"What payment options are available on the machine?"

"How has the district/school been affected by the vending guideline changes that have occurred in recent years?"

"How have you been handling the losses?"

"In what ways are you trying to recover lost revenue?"

"The White House is going to be tightening guidelines for snacks and drinks offered in vending machines at school. It is supposed to happen this year and the New York Times estimates that schools will lose a total of 2.3 billion dollars in vending machine sales annually. How are you going to offset your drop in revenue because of these changes?"

"What would you improve about your current vending's financial impact at your school?"

"If you asked your current vendor how healthy products would sell when mixed with unhealthy products, what do you think they would say?"

"How does your current vendor determine what products are healthy, tasty, and what your students will buy to help you drive your commissions?"

If after the opening question they answered health/wellness/education, he'd follow with these questions:

"Why is that area the most important to you?"

"How would you say your current vending is complementing your school's goal for cultivating a healthier environment?"

"How is your current vending situation helping you positively change student food choice behavior?"

"In what ways is your current vendor involving your students in nutrition education?"

"What were the deciding factors for districts'/schools' decision to remove/restrict vending?"

"How is your current machine(s) helping you encourage students to actually purchase and consume healthy snacks and drinks?"

"How is the current nutritional value of your vending affecting student behavior, attendance, and performance?"

"What would you improve about your current vending's nutritional and educational impact at your school?"

"What nutritious and performance-enhancing snack and drink options are available to your school's athletes?"

"How do think parents would react if they saw an interactive, educational, vending machine feeding their kids healthier snacks and drinks?"

If their first answer was ease/hassle free:

"Why is that area the most important to you?"

"How have stricter vending guidelines and revenue loss affected your daily responsibilities?"

"What would you change or improve about your current vending situation to make it easier for you to deal with?"

"How would you like to make your current vending more hassle-free?"

If Chad wasn't getting a good response, and/or determined there wasn't much interest from the prospect, he'd try some final questions to see if he could salvage something, or light a bit of a fire.

"How would you determine if it's worth it to look at some more information on a healthy vending program?"

"What results must a vending program produce for you to be open to looking additional information?"

If at some point they said, "they're satisfied," he'd reply with:

"What would it take for you to be more than satisfied?"

The Close

The primary objective was to ultimately get them to agree to the next meeting. After sufficiently determining their need and interest, Chad would ask for commitment with,

"Dr. Cook, it seems to me like we might have something here worth taking a look at. If there were a way for you to see some options that would help you to (benefit), (benefit), and (benefit) while making it as hassle-free as possible, would you be open to a conversation about some ideas?"

As you can see, this is definitely NOT an example of someone just smiling and dialing and playing the numbers. It is a case of a motivated sales professional willing to put the time in to follow a process, practice, and refine it. And, the results showed.

I checked in with Chad right before I turned in this chapter. He said,

As a young start-up some of our sales processes were still in development so we took Art's book, Smart Calling, and used that to build our sales foundation. It has become our go to source for all things sales-related and has enabled us to continue growing at an incredible pace. We'd recommend this book and Art's development process regardless of what you sell.

Smart Calling Makeovers

My websites always experience spikes in traffic when I post examples and recordings of calls I've received and those submitted by readers and customers. I attribute it to the *American Idol* phenomenon: In sort of a twisted way, people take some amount of joy in seeing and hearing others struggle and make fools of themselves.

Nevertheless, these calls are great learning tools. (You can hear examples of the calls I've already posted at my blog, www.SmartCalling.com. Go to the Call Recordings category.) Here are just a few of them.

Freight Industry Opening Statement

One particular caller sounded quite distressed as he explained, *"I'm an outside sales rep, and my teleprospector quit. So I have to do my own prospecting, and I hate it. I'm a good outside rep, but I'm freezing up when I have to call these people."*

"What are you saying to them?" I asked.

"I'm_____ with_____. We are a freight shipper, and I'd like to come out and take some of your time to explain what we do."

Analysis and Recommendation

No wonder he didn't like prospecting. I would have been paranoid, too, with the resistance he was surely getting from that opening. But it was entirely unnecessary—because like most resistance we encounter, he was creating it himself.

Because that opening was *awful*.

To paraphrase, it said, *"We're one of the hundreds of companies in this business. I want to show up at your office and take your valuable time so I can blab about my company and why I think we're good. It's all about me, you know."*

There is nothing of interest for the prospect here, no reason for him to even listen on that call, much less agree to an appointment. It puts the listener on the defensive, closes his mind to possibilities, and causes him to shift into his "Let's get this guy off the phone" mode.

This is a classic example of openings I often see and hear from sales reps who believe that they should get an appointment merely because they place a phone call. That's why they also feel they need to place 100 calls to get one appointment. I guess if you went to the mall and asked 100 people if they were interested in buying from you, you probably would bump into one who just might. That's not a particularly smart tactic, though. Why people would want to subject themselves to such a beating is beyond me. Doing and saying the *right things* minimize resistance and reap more success.

First, I suggested that he study all of the steps we covered in this book, especially identifying his Possible Value Propositions, since that was absent in this approach. Once that was done, he needed to do some pre-call intelligence research and social engineering to see what useful information he might be able to uncover. Ideally, he'd like to find prospects with dissatisfaction issues with the carriers they were currently using. I gave him a simple suggestion for an opening that could be modified and tailored with Smart information when it is collected:

> "I'm_____ with_____. In speaking with Mike, your dock manager, I understand you're anticipating a rush of scattered shipments over the next few months. We've worked with many traffic managers in the [fill in prospect's industry], helping them get the best rates and on-time deliveries with no hassles. Depending on what you ship, and to where, it might be worth our time to talk."

He liked it but mentioned it doesn't ask for the appointment right away.

Precisely. That is one of the mistakes I suggest you avoid. I asked if he ever had situations where he visited a so-called prospect who was less than euphoric about the appointment, conducted a lobby interview where they spoke as the prospect walked to his next task, or met with someone who really wasn't a prospect at all. Of course—many, he admitted.

So why even visit these people? Why not conduct the preliminaries by phone? If you're using the phone to prospect—regardless of whether your next step is to communicate in person—be certain you have something of interest in order to get prospects talking. Your results will be much more pleasurable and profitable.

A Mistake-Filled Call

Many sales reps look to ads, direct mailing pieces, catalogs, the Internet, or anywhere that advertising exists as sources of prospects. This is wise and a source of Smart Calling information. However, many of these reps stop there with their intelligence gathering. They do not effectively use what they learn and are therefore ill-prepared for what they inevitably hear on calls.

Here's an example of a call I received.

> *Caller:* "*Hello, this is Bill Jones with Video Recorders. I saw the promotion for your Telesales Success DVD videos and wanted you to know that we do DVD duplication.*"
>
> "*Okay.*"

He became flustered at this point, probably because I didn't say, "*Oh, you do DVD duplication? Where should I send my master copy? You can do mine.*"

> "Uh, I'd like to talk to you about doing yours."
>
> "Look, I'll save you some time. I selected my existing company after evaluating quite a few. They have a very good price, quality is fine, and service is great. I have no reason to even consider looking around."
>
> "Oh, okay. Keep us in mind."

Yeah, sure I will.

Analysis and Recommendations

You might be thinking that I gave this guy an iron-clad objection that would eliminate me forever as a prospect for him. And maybe you're right for the most part—when it comes to getting a sale on *that* call. However, he undoubtedly runs into that same objection quite a bit, so I'm surprised he hasn't learned to use something that won't totally slam the door so suddenly in his face. Here's what I would do, were I in his situation:

Call Strategy and Preparation

If I were placing this call, my primary objective would be to get commitment that the prospects would use my service the next time they had a DVD project. Although I wouldn't achieve this on a majority of the calls, it's always best to aim high. After realizing on the call this wouldn't be reached, objectives—in descending order—would be to get a commitment that I could at least bid on their next job and, if that wasn't met, to get agreement that they would at least keep us on file as a backup supplier in case their existing duplicator for some reason no longer met their needs. A bigger-picture, more strategic objective would be to identify their marketing plans and initiatives for the future and if they had other future projects coming up.

Preliminary Intelligence
This salesperson knew nothing about me when he called, other than the fact that he saw a promotion for some DVDs. He very easily could have seized the opportunity to ask the person who answered the phone here who we now use for duplication, how many we typically order, what we pay, what issues we run into, and any other qualifying information that would have better equipped him for the call. Plus, he would have learned *that* person—not me—is the one who actually deals with the duplicator regularly.

Opening Statement
He gave no reason for me to even listen. He may as well just said, "Well, I've finally called you, so I guess you can start using us now." Simply dialing the phone does not give a salesperson the right to take a prospect's time; promising or hinting at some value they could get does. I would have listened to something like this:

> *"I'm Bill Jones with Video Recorders. I see you are regularly producing training DVDs and understand that you feel you might be paying a premium for short runs. We specialize in top-quality DVD duplication and now work with quite a few training organizations, especially for smaller orders that require quick turnaround. Depending on the price you're now paying and your level of satisfaction with the quality and service you're getting, it might be worth it for you to take a look at a bid we could do for you."*

I would have been more likely to answer questions at this point. However, even if I did retort with the same early-resistance objection mentioned earlier, he could have picked up on it and used it to ask more questions, for example, *"I see. What price are you paying?"*

If that resulted in a dead end, a last resort question to at least try to accomplish the last chance objective would be *"What plans do you have in place for a backup supplier? If, for example, you needed a large quantity in a hurry and your supplier wasn't able to accommodate you for some reason?"*

Determine if any parts of your call process are similar to this one. Analyze every step of the process, home in on your strengths and enhance them, and shore up the weak areas.

Beware of the Bad Information Floating Around

Here's an opening statement suggestion I read from a sales trainer and author in an online article. It's no wonder so many people get beat up on the phone if they practice stuff like this, which is from a supposed expert. While there is a lot of free sales tips and information online, in many cases, that's exactly what it is worth.

> *"Hello, this is_____ with Reclamation Services. We specialize in commercial recycling services, and I'd like to ask you about your company's recycling policy. Do you have just a moment for a couple of quick questions?"*

I'm sure you can see the one glaring, critical component that is missing: *why* the person should take a moment to answer a couple of quick questions. Most busy people who very well might be great prospects see nothing of value in the call, and quickly exit. Even if someone actually *does* answer the questions in response to an opener like this, consider their frame of mind: They probably are bracing themselves for the sales pitch. They're tentative and skeptical as they answer the questions—not the desirable state of mind for people you'd like to persuade.

You can fix all of that by using the Smart Calling process in this book. Your opening must make them think that you might be able to do something for them. This sparks their curiosity and interest, earns you the right to take some of their time, and puts them in a more favorable frame of mind to answer your questions—since you've already hinted at the payoff for them. This missing component can very easily be added, combined with even the slightest bit of Smart information, making the example much more effective:

> *"Hello, this is_____ with Reclamation Services. I saw the news on your company blog about your new green initiative for next quarter. We specialize in commercial recycling services for the_____ industry, by helping companies reduce their trash-hauling expenses, and also cutting their costs on everyday paper goods, in some cases as much as 37 percent. If I've caught you at a good time, I'd like to ask you about your new recycling policy to see if this would be worth your taking a look at."*

ABOUT THE AUTHOR

Since he was 14 years old, in his first sales job on the phone selling tickets to the police fund-raising circus, Art Sobczak has been a student, practitioner, and, since 1983, a teacher of professional sales and prospecting using the phone.

All through high school and college he held a variety of jobs that allowed him to sit in the comfort of an office, making money for others and himself simply by talking on the phone. He knew he was onto something. That trend continued after college in corporate sales positions with the original AT&T and with a division of American Express.

Since forming his company, Business By Phone Inc., Art has helped hundreds of thousands of salespeople—and those who might not have considered themselves being in sales—to generate untold millions of dollars and extraordinary success by saying and doing the right things by phone using conversational, commonsense, nonsalesy processes and techniques.

He provides this assistance through many forms, including customized onsite training workshops, keynotes, and sales kickoffs for companies and associations (more than 1,500 delivered) and his public Telesales College two-day training seminars. In addition, he has authored more than 100 audio, video, and printed and electronic learning resources; for more than 29 years he has written and published the monthly *Telephone Prospecting and Selling Report* training newsletter, and for more than 13 years his free weekly sales tips e-zine.

In 2012 Art was recognized for his contribution to the inside sales profession by the American Association of Inside Sales Professionals with their Lifetime Achievement Award.

To contact Art about possibly customizing a Smart Calling workshop for your company or association, or any other type of inside sales training, e-mail him at ArtS@BusinessByPhone.com, or call (480) 699–0958.

Other Smart Calling and Inside Sales Resources

www.BusinessByPhone.com

Free weekly e-mail sales tips, free e-books and reports, and listing of Art's other books, audios, videos, events, and training resources. See information on Art's training programs and a demo video.

www.SmartCalling.com

Art's Smart Calling Blog, with updated Smart Calling tips, techniques, observations, call recordings, rants, and more.

www.SmartCallingOnline.com

Art's Inner Circle membership and coaching program where you can have personal access to him.

INDEX